Heroes, Legends, Champions

Heroes, Legends, Champions

Why Heroism Matters

Andrew Bernstein

UNION SQUARE
PUBLISHING

Published by
Union Square Publishing
301 E. 57th Street, 4th floor
New York, NY 10022
www.unionsquarepublishing.com

Manufactured in the United States of America, or in the
United Kingdom when distributed elsewhere.

Bernstein, Andrew
Heroes, Legends, Champions:
Why Heroism Matters
LCCN: 2019916626
ISBN: 978-1-946928-24-5
eBook: 978-1-946928-45-0

Cover design by: Joe Potter
Interior design: Medlar Publishing Solutions Pvt Ltd., India
Cover art: 'Triumph of Daedalus Over Fate and Futility'
by Bryan Larsen (www.bryanlarsen.com)

www.andrewbernstein.net

To Penelope Joy,
The Heroine of Her Own Life

Throughout history, in numerous forms, great heroes have been mankind's benefactors. They have created beautiful and inspiring works of art. They have cured diseases. They have identified the laws of logic, made scientific breakthroughs, and developed rational philosophy. They have won wars in defense of liberty. They have accomplished much more besides—and always, in so doing, they have overcome obstacles that would daunt a lesser man.

To the select few that have carried mankind forward, who, under arduous conditions, have created, and/or defended civilization.

"Never was so much owed by so many to so few."
Winston Churchill

Table of Contents

Introduction

Flourishing human life requires heroes.

The reasons for this are two: Heroes perform great deeds, such as exploring Earth's oceans and far flung continents, learning to grow crops and feed populations, protecting their homelands from foreign invaders, and much more. Further, they inspire us to seek the best within ourselves. Afterall, if a hero overcomes fearsome obstacles to achieve noteworthy goals, why cannot we surmount daunting challenges to fulfill our purposes?

The answer, of course, is that we can.

But, unfortunately, for the past century, serious culture, including the arts, has been dominated by an anti-hero mentality. Heroes, if they are presented at all—in literature or film, in history or biography—are persistently demeaned. In the name of "balance," contemporary thinkers feel compelled to harp upon a hero's flaws, whether real or imagined, proportionate or exaggerated, and to grant these equal weight to grand-scale achievement; as though, for example, Thomas Edison's neglect of his children were as worthy of notation as his life-giving accomplishments.

In truth, Edison's neglect of his children was a serious moral failing and, by us, it should be acknowledged and condemned. But after censuring the moral breach, we selectively focus on the grand-scale, life-giving accomplishments. A hero may be flawed, even morally so; but his life-advancing accomplishments might stand apart from and untarnished by the flaws. A hero may be heroic in respect of epic deeds accomplished, even though the rest of his life is mundane or even morally blemished. If so, we acknowledge and deplore the blemish. But we focus on and celebrate the epic deeds.

In life, that which advances life, not that which retards or undermines it, always warrants our most pronounced attention.

In honoring a hero, we perform an act of justice to one who merits it; we motivate future heroic deeds by showing that they will be rewarded; and, hopefully, we are ourselves inspired to strive more heroically in pursuit of life-enhancing goals.

The anti-heroes that dominate serious modern literature and film are hapless persons for whom we feel sympathy, not admiration. They are overcome by alcoholism, or drug addiction, or dysfunctional families, or listless ennui, and so forth. We feel for them—and, in real-life, strive to aid them.

But we need heroes—both real-life heroes and realistic fictional projections of them—not just super-powered comic book figures (the popularity of which shows how starved humanity is for the sight of heroism.) Now more than ever, in an intellectual culture that shuns serious heroes, we need an appreciation of them.

It is this truth that motivated me to write this book.

I was reared in a severely dysfunctional family in Brooklyn, New York, whose afflictions made it impossible for us to travel. I nurtured myself on the sight of heroes, real-life or fictional, in books, in film, in history, and in current events. I was aware that there is a wide world out there, and its possibilities fascinated me. "Aqaba is there," says T.E. Lawrence, pointing across the desert in the epic film, *Lawrence of Arabia.* "It is only a matter of going." But the Nefud Desert is presumed to be impassable, and going there—or many other places—is difficult and dangerous in the extreme.

Such daunting quests are the undertakings of heroes. In my youth and to the present, I especially gloried in the tales of great explorers and pioneers—of Magellan, for example, of Shackleton, of Amelia Earhart, of Jim Lovell, and of others.

I am an unabashed hero worshiper. Worship, properly understood, of life-giving heroes is a profoundly positive attribute. It has helped me overcome numerous life obstacles and it can similarly help many others.

And so this book was born. It is not a self-help book. Its purpose is to not to show us how to apply the lessons of a hero's life in our own. Rather, it is a theoretical book, explaining what heroes are and why mankind needs them. Before we can emulate heroes, we must properly identify them, we must understand who and what they are.... And what they are not. This is a matter of life and death. Some persons, for example, at various times have considered as heroes Adolf Hitler, Josef Stalin, and Osama bin Laden. If we are to promote human life, it is necessary for us to clearly understand that and why mass murderers are definitively excluded from the echelon of heroes.

Those interested in the topic of heroes may remember that this subject was hotly debated by such prominent 19th century thinkers as Thomas Carlyle, Herbert Spencer, William James, and Friedrich Nietzsche. Then, it was known as the "great man theory of history." Originally, I included in this book a chapter critiquing these thinkers and that theory. For the sake of brevity, I expunged it. But it remains a fascinating subject. For those who wish to explore that specific vision of heroes, I have posted the original chapter on my website as a stand-alone essay. It is entitled "The Great Man Theory of History" and is available, for free, at: www.andrewbernstein.net.

It is my hope that this book makes an original contribution to our understanding of heroes. But given such an extensive literature on the subject, an important question must be raised: Is there something new to be said regarding heroes?

Afterall, for millennia prior to the 20th century, human beings have glorified mighty, albeit diverse champions—from Achilles in *The Iliad*, to Rostand's Cyrano, to numerous other fictional projections, to countless real-life, larger-than-life instances. Much dialogue has ensued and vast quantities of ink employed in an effort to uncover the nature of this phenomenon.

With much respect to numerous predecessors, I believe there remain important truths to be discovered regarding heroism.

The first questions are: What is a hero? What makes someone a hero?

Or: How do we distinguish a hero from a non-hero?

Popular Definitions of Hero

We can, of course, start with a good dictionary. *The American Heritage Dictionary*, 5th Edition, defines "hero" as: 1. "In mythology and legend, a man, often of divine ancestry, who is endowed with great courage and strength, celebrated for his bold exploits, and favored by the gods. 2. A person noted for feats of courage or nobility of purpose, especially one who has risked or sacrificed his or her life: *soldiers and nurses who were heroes in an unpopular war*. 3. A person noted for special achievement in a particular field: *the heroes of medicine*."

The first definition associates heroes often with gods and myths. Of course, a "legend" could be a real person, for example, Leonidas I, warrior King of Sparta, who led the Greek resistance to Persian invasion at Thermopylae, and subsequently achieved an immortal fame for prowess and bravery. Still, this definition errs in its reliance on mythical beings.

But its main problem is that in most myths and legends, the characteristics prized as "heroic" were generally martial prowess and physical bravery, for example, Achilles. Indeed, the definition's mention of strength most likely denotes bodily, not intellectual and/or moral strength. This first definition, then, is either non-literal, linking heroes to myths and men of divine provenance, or, at best, is too narrow, limiting them to mighty warriors.

The second definition, in its emphasis on risking or sacrificing one's life, construes "courage" in a limited sense, as largely a matter of risking one's life for a noble purpose. While such physical courage may certainly be characteristic of a hero, his/her courage can take different forms. Is it not possible that, in standing up for a noble cause, a hero can risk losing his love, his career, his freedom, his wealth, or another significant value, something distinct from life itself but still of great importance?

The third definition has much to recommend it. Its mention of "special achievement in a particular field" neither associates itself with myths nor limits itself to warriors or physical bravery. Related: Its example of "the heroes of medicine" properly emphasizes the potential role of intellect in a hero's make-up. Nevertheless, as stated, "special achievement" is vague and in need of explication.

The dictionary definitions in this case prove of limited value. We need a better method of identifying the characteristics that make someone a hero.

Another possibility is to examine a range of persons, either fictional or real-life, generally considered to be heroes, and discover whether study of their exploits yields productive insight. However, there is a pitfall to be avoided in this approach.

For if we consider someone a hero—George Washington, let us say—and then extract the characteristics of heroism from examination of his life, the question that emerges is: How did we know he was a hero in the first place? Afterall, we seek the defining characteristics of a hero. In the absence of such knowledge, we could not yet identify who is or is not one.

Can this problem—known in Logic as question-begging—be avoided? Can an examination of individuals generally considered heroes yield fruitful results? In this specific form—no, it cannot. For the reason stated above, this method is doomed to failure. We need a better method of identifying the nature of a hero.

It is one purpose of this book to provide it.

Finally, a word on the book's structure.

Chapters One, Two, and Three focus on the nature and definition of a hero, and provide a method for distinguishing a hero from non-heroes. Chapter Four raises the question of whether, under appropriate circumstances, everyman and everywoman can rise to heroic heights—and answers in the affirmative. Chapter Five discusses an appropriate response to morally-flawed heroes. Chapters Six, Seven, and Eight dispute the conventional notion that heroism involves self-sacrifice and demonstrate, rather, that heroism, properly understood, involves actions self-fulfilling; heroism and self-sacrifice are, in fact, moral antagonists. Chapter Nine explains the errors of the modern antihero mentality. Finally, Chapter Ten shows the life-giving importance of hero worship. The two appendices validate philosophic principles that underlie the theory of heroes elucidated here: That human life is the standard of moral value and that human beings possess free will.

I gratefully acknowledge my philosophic indebtedness to Ayn Rand and to her leading student, Dr. Leonard Peikoff. Any errors committed here in applying Ayn Rand's theories are entirely my own. I wish to thank Dr. Bradley Thompson, head of the Clemson Institute for the Study of Capitalism at Clemson University, for hiring me to write this book. My year at Clemson was outstanding. Craig Biddle, publisher and editor of the superb journal, *The Objective Standard*, aided significantly in the editing of this book; as did philosophy professor, Alan Wachtel. Carl Barney, both a self-made man and a real-life hero, contributed in several forms to the funding of this book. And, finally, my beautiful daughter, Penelope Joy, provided her daddy endless amounts of inspiration.

Andrew Bernstein
New York, NY
September, 2019

CHAPTER ONE

A Series of Striking Stories

Let us begin with a number of vivid tales, of both fictional and real-life persons.

One: Shane

Jack Schaefer's classic Western novel, *Shane*, tells the story of a noble gunfighter who seeks to hang up his guns, to retire from his bloody profession, and to lead a peaceful existence.

Shane, dressed all in black, rides alone into a frontier valley of the 19th century American West. He believes he can start a new, non-violent life.

But range war brews in this seemingly peaceful valley—and Shane rides into the midst of a conflict simmering between ranchers and farmers.

Cattle barons had originally settled the land and wrested it, in fierce combat, from the grasp of warlike tribes. They let their cattle roam across the range. Subsequently, farmers moved into the valley, grew crops, and fed them to their steers, raising fatter cattle in the process. They fenced off their property and, in some instances, deprived the cattle barons' steers access to streams. Range war, in this small

Wyoming valley—far from the nearest outpost of law enforcement—is inescapable.

A leader of the farmers is a hard-working, productive family man of great personal integrity—Joe Starrett. He and his wife, Marian, have a young son, Bobby, who is reared to be, like his father, an upright man of peaceful productivity.

Shane, the soft-spoken stranger, says nothing about his past and carries no gun, but the fluid grace with which he moves and the mystery surrounding his slim, black-garbed frame combine to manifest both a superlative physical prowess and an air of silent menace. One day, Bobby overhears an old mule-skinner describe Shane: "He's like one of these here slow-burning fuses.... Quiet and no sputtering. So quiet you forget it's burning. Then it sets off one heck of a blow-off of trouble when it touches powder. That's him." Marian says regarding the incognito gunfighter: "More than [mysterious]. Dangerous." Joe responds: "He's dangerous, all right.... But not to us, my dear.... In fact, I don't think you ever had a safer man in your house."

These truths begin becoming apparent when Shane signs on as Joe's hired hand. Although Joe is a massive barrel-chested specimen and Shane shorter and slighter, the smaller man pulls an equal weight when they uproot a massive tree trunk on the Starrett property. Further, when Shane, on a trip to town, is assailed by hands of the leading cattle baron, Fletcher, he single-handedly punches out a small posse of them, before Joe arrives to mop up the rest.

Shane's lithe figure, moving with the grace of a silent predator, generates immense power.... for either construction or for destruction.

He and the family form an immediate bond: Bobby idolizes him. Marian is stirred. Joe tells her he understands, for Shane is a better man.

Fletcher realizes that neither Shane nor Starrett can be physically bullied. He hires a murderous gunslinger, Stark Wilson, to intimidate the farmers. Wilson, in cold blood, guns down one of Starrett's fellow farmers. Fletcher, with his hired gun, rides to Starrett's farm to make a final offer: He will hire both Shane and Starrett, Joe and Marian can retain their farm, but the other farmers must go. He gives Starrett the night to think about it. Starrett wavers, for he seeks to endanger neither his family nor Shane.

Joe will go alone into town to negotiate with Fletcher. But if he rejects Fletcher's offer, the cattle baron will likely have Wilson gun him down.

Shane takes the deadly situation into his own hands.

Whipping a pistol across the side of Joe's head, he knocks the bigger man out, thereby keeping him safe at home. Then, alone, he rides to town. But now, he wears a beautiful, ivory-plated pistol in a soft leather holster near to his right hand. Bobby thinks:

"Belt and holster and gun ... These were not things he was wearing or carrying. They were part of him, part of the man, of the full sum of the integrate force that was Shane. You could see now that for the first time this man who had been living with us, who was one of us, was complete, was himself in the final effect of his being."

He rides into town, Bobby racing secretly after him. Shane enters the crowded barroom.

"Where's Fletcher?" he calls.

He receives no answer—only the "lazy and insolent" voice of the killer, Wilson: "Where's Starrett?"

Shane comes down the center aisle of the saloon. Wilson is by the door, his back to the wall, directly in front of him. Shane speaks gently to the killer: "I had a few things to say to Fletcher ... That can wait. You're a pushing man, Wilson, so I reckon I had better accommodate you." Wilson replies he has no quarrel with Shane—it is Starrett he wants. Shane responds: "What you want, Wilson, and what you'll get are two different things. Your killing days are done."

Wilson goes for his gun. He fires across the room. Shane fires back. Both gunfighters are wounded, Shane in his side, Wilson in his right arm. The killer's hand is numbed, he drops the gun. With his left, he reaches for his other weapon and draws the gun. Shane shoots him in the chest, killing him. Then, a shot is fired from the balcony, the bullet whipping through Shane's shirt. Shane whirls, he dives, he fires, his shot catches Fletcher in the act of re-aiming, and the cattle baron keels over the railing and collapses, dead, to the floor. Bobby describes it vividly:

"I saw the whole man move, all of him, in the single flashing instant. I saw the head lead and the body swing and the driving power of the legs beneath. I saw the arm leap and the hand take the gun in the lightning sweep. I saw the barrel line up like—like a finger pointing—and the flame spurt even as the man himself was still in motion.

"And there on the balcony Fletcher, impaled in the act of aiming for a second shot, rocked on his heels and fell back..."

Shane is bleeding and his energy begins to flag. But then a strange thing happens. Bobby, in hiding, says:

"How could one describe it, the change that came over him? Out of the mysterious resources of his will the vitality came. It came creeping, a tide of strength that crept through him and fought and shook off the weakness. It shone in his eyes and they were alive again and alert. It welled up in him, sending that familiar power surging through him again until it was singing again in every vibrant line of him."

Gently, he warns the men in the bar: "I'll be riding on now. And there's not a one of you that will follow."

In magnificent isolation, he rides away, permanently alienated from the peaceful family he loves by the violent act that saves them.

Bobby, in hiding, had witnessed the climactic gunfight. He wants to believe in the invincible prowess of the hero he worships. He races out into the street and gets to Shane in time.

"'I don't care,' I said, the tears starting. 'I don't care if he was the fastest that ever was. He'd never have been able to shoot you, would he? You'd have got him straight, wouldn't you—if you had been in practice?' He hesitated a moment. He gazed down at me and into me and he knew. He knew what goes on in a boy's mind and what can help him stay clean inside through the muddled, dirtied years of growing up. 'Sure. Sure, Bob. He'd never even have cleared the holster.'"

The boy wants the savior of his family to stay. But Shane, revealed now to be a consummate gunfighter, has other thoughts. "A man is what he is, Bob, and there's no breaking the mold. I tried that and I've lost. But I reckon it was in the cards from the moment I saw a freckled kid on a rail up the road there and a real man behind him, the kind that could back him for the chance another kid never had."

He rides into the night of the vast American West, consciously choosing to leave the child to grow up with his parents and to emulate his honest, hard-working, peaceful father. Later that night, a witness of the gunfight says to Starrett: "He's [Shane's] alive all right. Wilson got to him. But no bullet can kill that man.... Sometimes I wonder whether anything ever could."

Later, alone with his mother, Bobby tells her everything he saw. "I told her, and when I was done, all she said in a soft little murmur was 'Thank you.' She looked out the window and murmured the words again and they were not for me and she was still looking out over the land to the great gray mountains when finally I fell asleep."

As the time went by, the stories of Shane were told and re-told in the valley, each embellishment more outlandish than those previous. But Bobby paid no heed. For he knew the truth: "He was the man who rode into our little valley out of the heart of the great glowing West and when his work was done rode back whence he had come and he was Shane."

Two: Maria Montessori

The future trailblazer in childhood education was born in a provincial Italian town in 1870. From the beginning, she overturned conventions. She read widely and deeply, an unusual quality for Italian women of her day. When she was thirteen she enrolled in an all-male technical institute, studying for a future career as an engineer. She changed her mind, however, and decided to attend medical school and become a physician.

But at that time, there were few female medical doctors in Italy, and the prejudices of the day led to stubborn opposition from diverse quarters: Professors, medical schools, even family members sought to discourage her. She was, at first, denied admission to medical school. But she was not one to relent. Persevering, when 20 years old, she entered a natural sciences program at the University of Rome, where she studied general and organic chemistry, experimental physics, zoology, anatomy, and botany. Graduating from this program qualified her to attend medical school. The website of the American Montessori Society states: "With great effort, she gained admittance, opening the door a bit wider for future women in the field."

Because of her gender, she was faced with animosity from both students and professors: As but one example, she was barred from performing dissections of cadavers with the men, permitted to effect them only when alone. Nevertheless, she triumphed over these impediments: In her first year she won an academic prize, in 1896 she graduated from the University of Rome with a doctorate in medicine, and the following year she succeeded in publishing her doctoral thesis.

But then arose other obstacles to be overcome.

For a number of years she worked with and researched children who had been dubbed by social institutions "slow" or "retarded." She and a fellow doctor, Giuseppe Montesano, were co-directors of the Orthophrenic School of Rome. She fell in love with him—and the result of their love was her only child, their son, Mario Montessori, born in 1898. But if she married, she would be expected to retire from her work and be a full-time wife and mother. But she would not—could not—give up her work with the children. Rather, she preferred to keep her relationship with Montesano secret, under the condition that neither of them would ever marry another. When he united with another woman, she felt betrayed; she left the university hospital and placed their son in foster care.

The mores of the day, in effect, required her to choose between career and family, costing her both the man she loved and estrangement from her son during his early life. (Although she and Mario were re-united during his teenage years, and he subsequently worked with her closely for many years.)

Her work with the special needs children enabled them to make cognitive progress unexpected by the educational establishment. It also provided her an opportunity to begin rudimentary development of the methods and materials that, later, would constitute the Montessori revolution in education.

Around this time, in 1906–07, she was invited to oversee the education of working class children in a poor neighborhood in Rome. She accepted and, so, the first *Casa de Bambini* or Children's House was born. She innovated across a wide range of methods and topics: She replaced the heavy, adult-size furniture with lighter, smaller, child-size models, she developed learning materials of a size appropriate to children and placed them on shelves sufficiently low for young children to readily access, she emphasized the development of a child's sensory observation as the foundation of learning, she noticed and respected that children were naturally eager learners, she stressed the importance of each individual human being, she encouraged students to pursue their own loves with the materials and the subjects that especially fascinated them, and she came to realize that developing independent thinking was the most important goal of education.

Her fame as an expert educator spread across Italy and then throughout many parts of the globe. She wrote books, she traveled and lectured widely, including in the United States. By 1911–12, the Montessori method was becoming popular in the U.S. *McLure's Magazine*, a popular journal of the day, ran a series of articles on it. In 1911, the first American Montessori school opened in Tarrytown, New York. Alexander Graham Bell, inventor of the telephone, supported her methods—and her book, *The Montessori Method*, sold widely in the U.S. She visited the United States on a lecture tour in late-1913 and was greeted everywhere by large, energetic audiences. By 1913, there were one hundred Montessori schools in operation in the country.

During this same period, she was able to successfully initiate her educational methods in Spain, the Netherlands, and the United Kingdom, as well.

But then, in the 1920s, Benito Mussolini, the Fascist leader, came to power in Italy. Surprisingly, initially, the dictator supported her work, establishing a Montessori teacher training college and backing a number of Italian Montessori schools.

But trouble with the Fascists was inescapable.

She clashed with Mussolini's regime over several issues, including philosophic ones, especially after she began lecturing on the relationship between education and peace. By 1932, she and her son were placed under state surveillance and, in 1934, she left her native land. By 1936, the Fascist regime had ended all Montessori education in Italy.

Her biographer wrote: "When the Fascist rule became dominant in Italy, she came to realize that an education which had as its aim the development of a strong and free personality could not thrive in a totalitarian atmosphere. Indeed, the Fascists ordered all her schools to be shut down. In Germany and Austria—then under Nazi rule—things were even more drastic. An effigy of Montessori was burned over a pyre of her own books in a public square both in Berlin and Vienna."[1]

Making matters worse, when World War II broke out, she and her son were in British-controlled India. As citizens of Italy, the two were considered enemy aliens by the British, who interned Mario for two months and subsequently confined the two to an Indian compound for the war's duration.

Years earlier, her educational theories had come under attack by rival educators in the United States. William Heard Kilpatrick, for example, a leading supporter of John Dewey's Progressive school of education, wrote a sharply critical book entitled, *The Montessori Method Examined,* and the National Kindergarten Association likewise censured her methods. Combined with Montessori's insistence on maintaining strict quality control over methods, materials, and teacher training, these and other criticisms led to a splintering of support and a decline of American interest in her system.

But a good deal changed in the period between the end of World War II and the years surrounding her death in 1952. She left India, returned to Europe and, despite her advanced age, continued the educational struggle. She traveled and lectured, she wrote books, and worked tirelessly for her educational cause: the training of a child's independent thinking.

By our day, her long struggle to revolutionize childhood education came to bear substantial fruit: The 1950s saw a revival of American interest in her methods and, internationally, there are a total of 22,000 Montessori schools in roughly 110 countries.

Montessori's method of training a child's cognitive capacity is of especial import in the United States, where, for large swathes of the 20th century, numerous educational professionals opposed the widespread teaching of an academic program.

Though often categorized jointly as "Progressives," they differed widely regarding their positive preferences: Some favored vocational training and preparation for the job market; some—including the aforementioned William Heard Kilpatrick—supported group work projects, where children learned to get along with others and, if necessary, conform to the group; yet others, admiring (and visiting) the Soviet Union, held that the purpose of education was to promote social change, to eradicate capitalism and install socialism, to teach children to not seek their own "selfish" ends but, rather, to serve the state; and so forth.

What they shared in common was an entrenched hostility to academic training.

Educational historian, Diane Ravitch, points out: "Progressive reformers believed that the scientific movement in education had ... demolished the rationale for the academic curriculum. They agreed that the academic curriculum was archaic.... Unthinkable ... [the] claim that the fundamental purpose of education was intellectual training."[2]

An egregious decline of the American educational system was a predictable result of their influence.[3]

But parents, most often wiser than so-called "educational experts," generally desire their children to excel in reading, writing, literature, mathematics, history, and the sciences. Not surprisingly, Montessori education made a sweeping comeback in America in the second half of the 20th century and, today, there are approximately 4,000 certified Montessori schools in the nation.

Maria Montessori's commitment to developing a child's mind—his/her capacity for independent critical thinking—is essential to a proper cognitive method; and all the more valuable in America, where it has been so long and strenuously opposed by myriad grandees of the nation's educational establishment.

Three: George Washington Carver

The agricultural revolutionary was born into slavery in Kansas during the U.S. Civil War, in a year of which historians are uncertain—and, as a child and young man, faced down a series of tribulations sufficient to dismay an individual of lesser internal fortitude.

First, while still an infant, he, a sister, and their mother were kidnapped by racist nightriders from Arkansas and were to be re-sold to new "owners," most likely "down the river" in the Deep South. His "owner," Moses Carver, was able to locate and re-purchase him from the raiders, but was unable to discover the whereabouts of George's mother or sister.

The young child never saw his mother again.

Additionally, young Carver was afflicted with a sickly constitution: He suffered from a severe case of whooping cough and frequent bouts with what was diagnosed as croup, an illness caused by a virus that makes a child's airways swell and results in a distinctive barking cough. His vocal cords were ripped from incessant coughing and, at times, he appeared to be at death's door but some inner toughness in his tiny frame prevented his succumbing.

Above all, seeking an education, he overcame a series of pervasively daunting obstacles in a titanic struggle that virtually defies credibility.

After his mother's kidnapping, Moses and Susan Carver reared young George as though he were their own son. He was a precocious child, hungry for knowledge, and "Aunt Susan" taught him to read and write. But his impassioned quest for learning soon outstripped the ability of his adopted parents to teach him.

He roamed the woods near the Carver farm, marveling at the diversity of the animate world: "Why did the night crawlers flee from the sun's warmth? And why couldn't the lilies survive without it? Why did roots that looked exactly the same produce an astonishing array of different-colored flowers?"[4] He had an endless series of questions to which he yearned for answers.

He hungered to attend the local elementary school, a one-room cabin in the nearby village of Locust Grove. As a young child, he would sit outside, on the doorstep, and listen to the students recite their lessons. Eagerly, he asked "Uncle Moses" when he would be old enough to attend school. Poor Moses Carver was confounded.

"How do you crush a dream gently [he wondered]? How do you tell a boy bursting with his newfound hunger to learn that though the slaves were free, and though Missouri law now proclaimed that 'no Negro should know any master, only God,' George could *never* go to the Locust Grove school, nor to any school for white children."[5]

Young George was shocked. What bearing did skin color have on the eagerness or ability to learn? In the world of nature he so passionately loved, some roses were yellow and some red—but both were roses. The sun shined, he knew, and the rain fell on all plants and flowers, regardless of color. Why should it be different for human beings? Internally, such rejection made him feel like he had been kicked in the stomach.

But he refused to relinquish his dream.

At roughly fourteen years of age, with the blessing of his adopted parents, George left home, and walked eight miles to Neosho, the county seat, to attend the school for black children. With no money and no place to stay, he slept the first night in a barn. He was taken in by a washerwoman, Mariah Watkins, and her husband for whom he performed odd jobs while attending school.

The school was housed in a flimsy, single-room shanty with cracked walls that, all through the winter, were inadequate to inhibit the biting wind that blew through the crevices. The children, wrapped in coats and mittens, shivered nevertheless, and young George's still-sickly frame was, again and again, afflicted with upper respiratory infections that prevented school attendance. Despite these impediments, George quickly exceeded the schoolteacher's knowledge and knew that, if he were to fulfill his dreams, it was time to move on.

Mariah Watkins said of him: "That boy told me he came to Neosho to find out what made hail and snow, and whether a person could change the color of a flower by changing the seed.... I told him he'd never find all that out in Neosho, nor in Joplin, either, and maybe not even in Kansas City. But all the time I knew he'd find it out—somewhere."[6]

But Carver's arduous struggle for education was barely begun.

He hitched a ride on a wagon bound for Fort Scott, Kansas, where he worked odd jobs, cooking, cleaning, and scrubbing linens, raising scant amounts of precious money with which to finance brief snatches of schooling. Fort Scott had been a hotbed of Southern sympathizers during the Civil War and anti-black prejudice still was rampant. One day, hefting in his arms his hard-earned school books, George was accosted by several white men. They cuffed him in the head, knocked him to the dirt, and stole his precious books ... because, in their ignorant view, "Negroes shouldn't go to school." Not a single one of the passersby interceded on the teenager's behalf.

Far worse, he later witnessed a lynch mob drag a black man from a wooden jail, beat him bloody, light a roaring bonfire in a public square, drench the victim in oil, and heave him, bleeding and begging, into the roaring flames. Townspeople watched, hoisted their children to better observe the spectacle, and neither civilians nor law men intervened to restrain the grisly murder.[7]

Before the next dawn, sick in his soul, George Carver fled Fort Scott, Kansas.

For ten years, Carver wandered the American West, performing odd jobs, searching for the nearest school, studying when he could, incessantly seeking wisdom, and hoping that this would be the year he finally completed seventh grade. By now, he was a bony six feet tall, stooped from ceaseless labors, but perennially undeterred. In Olathe, Kansas, he found a home for a time period sufficient to finish grade school. In Minneapolis, Kansas, in the first half of the 1880s, he opened a thriving laundry and attended a legitimate high school. In 1885, he was accepted into Highland College in Highland, Kansas.

Fall classes were to start on September 20th. He spent most of the summer studying typing and shorthand at a business academy in Kansas City. By August, he gained a job at a telegraph office, typing messages until midnight. As the time for college neared, he took a train to Joplin, then walked the thirteen miles to Neosho to bade farewell to Mariah Watkins. He then walked eight miles to Locust Grove for a nostalgic visit with his now-aged Uncle Moses Carver and an ailing Aunt Susan. After several days, he spent almost the entirety of his remaining money on a train ticket for Highland.

Arriving, he presented himself at the college and waited to see the Principal, the Reverend Duncan Brown. College—at last! The possibilities were boundless, the horizons stretched before him, the cultivation of wisdom would now be realized. Then he stood before Reverend Brown.

The clergyman's mouth spoke from a pinched face: "You didn't tell me you were Negro. Highland College does not take Negroes."

He was most likely, now, in his mid-twenties and had just been able to complete high school. This hammer blow to the solar plexus might have finished the educational quest of a lesser man. But if one expected that, one did not know George Carver.

Penniless, he slept that night in a barn and, in the morning, found a job on a fruit farm, pruning trees, cooking, and mending fences. He moved westward and, for two years, homesteaded on the Great Plains, where he built for himself a sod house and fought to preserve tenuous crops through furious blizzards and blazing summer sun. In 1888, he mortgaged his homestead for several hundred dollars and moved east.

Not far from Des Moines, Iowa, he finally caught a break. He got a job as a cook in a small town hotel and, in a local church, befriended the town doctor and his wife, who quickly recognized the young black man's extraordinary aptitude and burning desire. They recommended him to Simpson College in nearby Indianola, Iowa, a Methodist school founded on the principle that all men are created equal. On September 9, 1890, he set out on the thirty-mile walk to Indianola.

Probably age twenty-nine, George Carver was finally accepted into college.

A teacher wrote of him: "He came to Indianola with a satchel full of poverty and a burning zeal to know everything."

At Simpson, he enrolled in classes to study etymology, grammar, composition, and mathematics. He was an extraordinarily gifted artist with a deep yearning to paint, who excelled in his art courses at Simpson. But he loved plants, flowers, and horticulture with equal zeal. At some point he would have to choose. However, at long last, good fortune smiled on him. His art teacher, Etta Budd, recognized his prodigious, multi-talented gifts and recommended him to her father, Joseph Budd, Professor of Horticulture at the Iowa State Agricultural College (later to become Iowa State University) in Ames.

Around the turn of the 20th century, there was nowhere in the world an agricultural institution better stocked with brilliant minds, experimental methods, and revolutionary ideas than the sprawling campus in Ames.

Finally, the agricultural prodigy had been welcomed into the scientific promised land.

Carver, the first black student enrolled at Iowa State, received both his bachelor's and his master's degree at that institution, earning the latter in 1896.

If Carver had done nothing else in his life but overcome both racist foes and daunting obstacles to gain an outstanding education, his story would still be extraordinary. But, of course, we know of his monumental struggle because of the great achievements to come in agricultural science.

Hired by Booker T. Washington at Tuskegee Institute in 1896, he lived and worked there until his death in 1943. This part of his story is well-documented: At Tuskegee, he helped pioneer the principle and practice of crop rotation, teaching farmers methods to replenish their soil with nutrients. He developed peanuts and sweet potatoes into leading crops. Over the decades at Tuskegee, he taught numerous young black students, seeking to instill in them love of nature and scientific study. He traveled the countryside in his self-named "Jesup wagon," bringing his agricultural expertise to rural farmers, both black and white. From 1923 until 1933, he toured white Southern colleges, representing the Commission on Interracial Cooperation, speaking on behalf of racial amity. He dedicated his life and, upon his death, his savings to scientific research.

The epitaph on his tombstone at Tuskegee reads: "He could have added fortune to fame, but caring for neither, he found happiness and honor in being helpful to the world."

Carver did more than educate black college students, develop foodstuffs, increase agricultural production, instruct Southern farmers, and speak for racial harmony. He served as a role model for a generation of young, aspiring black American scientists; and his genius, his indomitable spirit, and his undying goodwill serve as a permanent inspiration, ecumenically, to human beings across the country and around the globe.

Four: Ernest Shackleton

Where Montessori and Carver triumphed over baleful social foes, Shackleton engaged in a desperate struggle for physical survival against inexorably potent natural forces.

Born in Ireland in 1874 to Anglo-Irish parents, Shackleton was a principal figure of the Heroic Age of Antarctic Exploration. He had been to Antarctica previously, including with lionized British polar explorer, Robert Falcon Scott, where he had already attained numerous accomplishments; but the staggering exploits upon which his reputation rests began in August, 1914, at the very start of World War I, when his ship, *Endurance*, departed British waters.

The great Norwegian explorer, Roald Amundsen, became the first man to reach the South Pole in 1911. So Shackleton, burning with desire to create an exalted legacy, set his sights on a different task: To become the first man to traverse the Antarctic land mass via crossing the South Pole.

Shackleton and his party, on board the *Endurance*, departed South Georgia Island, off the South America coast, on December 5. They encountered difficulties from the start: Deep in the Weddell Sea, off the coast of Antarctica, they navigated through thick ice floes … until they could proceed no farther. By January 19, 1915, the *Endurance* was stuck fast, unable to move under its own power, held captive in massive ice floes.

Shackleton's team was trapped on floating ice, slowly drifting northward, away from their destination.

Spring arrived in September and the breaking ice remorselessly staved in the ship's hull. She started taking on water on October 24, forcing the men to abandon ship and set up camp on the ice. On November 21, their ship sank.

Trapped on the ice floe, Shackleton hoped that they would drift toward Paulet Island, roughly 250 miles away, where they knew supplies had been stored. But on April 9, 1916, their ice floe split in two, and Shackleton commanded the men to launch the lifeboats, venturing to sea, heading for the nearest land. For five harrowing days, they battled sea, wind, and numbing cold before reaching Elephant Island, some 340 miles from where *Endurance* sank.

When the party waded ashore, it was the first time they had stood on solid ground in 497 days.

But Elephant Island was a deserted, barren outpost, wind-swept and bitterly cold, far from the main shipping lanes, offering little hope of either shelter or rescue. Shackleton knew they could not hope to long survive there. They had to risk crossing some 800 miles of tempest-tossed ocean in a small, open boat.

He chose five volunteers for the daunting journey to South Georgia Island, where an established whaling station offered haven. They out-fitted the lifeboat, *James Caird*, for the journey, and on April 24 they launched.

For fifteen days, exposed to the elements, they battled wind, current, and stormy seas, in constant peril of capsizing. They sailed through the Drake Passage, the most dreaded part of the Earth's massive oceans, where the winds often howled at hurricane velocities, at times gusting to 150 or even 200 miles per hour. Every ninety seconds or so, wind-whipped waves of fifty-foot size loomed behind their tiny craft, threatening to inundate them under millions of tons of sea water. The cold was bitter and they were constantly soaked.

They could not even think of South Georgia Island, for it seemed too remote.

"Instead, life was reckoned in periods of a few hours, or possibly only a few minutes—an endless succession of trials leading to deliverance from the particular hell of the moment."[8] Frank Worsley, skipper of the *Endurance*, said: It was "our baptism—the beginning of the ordeal by water."

In the bitter cold, ice formed athwart the vessel, covering the sails, as well as the oars, and at one point "the entire boat above the waterline was encased in ice, half a foot thick in places, and the rope to the sea anchor had grown to the size of a man's thigh. Under the weight of it, she was riding at least four inches deeper, like a waterlogged derelict rather than a boat."[9] Again and again, with axes, as frigid waves burst over them, they took turns chipping and chopping at the lethal ice whose dead weight could push them deeper and deeper into the sea.

On the eleventh day, May 4th, at midnight, a new enemy swept suddenly over them, a giant rogue wave, hissing, roaring, bearing down on them from astern. "And then it hit—and she was caught in a mountain of seething water and catapulted forward and sideways at the same time. She seemed actually to be thrown into the air.... For an instant, nothing existed but water. They couldn't even tell whether she was upright. But then the instant was over; the wave had rolled on..."[10] leaving the *Caird* filled with sea water reaching to the seats, unable to survive one more such blow, and the men bailed for their lives with any instrument that came to hand.

Tribulations mounted. Their fresh water was brackish from seawater seepage and barely drinkable. Foggy conditions set in, so that accurate sightings became near impossible. If they missed South Georgia in the fog, they could never beat back to it. Three thousand miles of Atlantic Ocean would then lie between them and the coast of Africa.

If they were on course, they should have been drawing nearer. If they had not passed it in the night, they should be only miles away and the towering peaks of South Georgia visible. The fear that they had missed it was palpable—missed it, with only thousands of miles of sea ahead of them ... and certain death. "Land!" a crew member finally cried. And then, Shackleton was the only one who spoke. "We've done it," he said.

But joy was short-lived, for new dangers awaited. A storm mounted, and the surging wind and heavy seas, if a landing were attempted, would have smashed them to pieces. They struggled through the night to keep their tiny craft from being dashed against the reefs. Worsley thought of the pity of it all: He had kept a diary for the entire seventeen months since *Endurance* had sailed—it was wrapped in rags and, although soaking wet, stowed in the vessel's forepeak. He was now too exhausted to fear death—but nobody would ever know how brutally close they had come.

But the storm abated, the wind somewhat slowed, and they spotted a narrow opening through a reef. They then landed, finally, back on South Georgia Island, some 522 days after they had departed.

But a towering new problem confronted them. The life boat had lost its rudder in the struggle against the elements and, overall, was unseaworthy. They were across South Georgia Island from the whaling station they sought. Between them and refuge lay 29 miles of 10,000 foot snow-capped peaks. One mountaineer had described the island as "a saw-tooth thrust through the tortured upheaval of mountain and glacier that falls in chaos to the northern sea." In the roughly 75 years that human beings had visited or resided on this island, no man had ever traversed the interior peaks, and for a simple reason—it could not be done.

But there was no other way.... and so began the ordeal by land.

With two companions, leaving the others behind in camp, Shackleton started up the slopes. They crawled up vertical icy peaks, cutting out steps with a carpenter's axe. They had no charts or maps of the interior, and had to guide themselves by sight. They had neither sleeping bags nor tents, because sleep in the frigid temperatures of those elevations meant certain death. They were not expert mountaineers, because they were seamen and Antarctic explorers. They carried only a small supply of food.

Time and again, after a grueling climb, they summited a steep peak.... only to find that either they had gone the wrong way or that there was no way down. Repeatedly, they retraced their steps, down the treacherously icy peaks, discouraged and exhausted.

Once, the only way down was to toboggan on their buttocks. What was far in the descending distance, they could not know. If they smashed into a boulder or flew off a precipice, they were gone. But staying at their current elevation or slowly descending via axe-carved steps meant fatal exposure in threadbare clothing to numbing cold. So they coiled up their rope to form a mat—they locked their arms and legs around each other—and, immediately, Shackleton kicked off.

"They seemed to hang poised for a split second, then suddenly the wind was shrieking in their ears, and a white blur of snow tore past. Down ... Down ... They screamed—not in terror necessarily, but simply because they couldn't help it. It was squeezed out of them by the rapidly mounting pressure in their ears and against their chests. Faster and faster—down ... down ... down!"[11]

They survived the mad descent.

They climbed more icy peaks. Again, in the absence of maps, they went in a wrong direction and were forced to retrace their steps. Once they had to rope their way down through the frigid waters of a 25-foot waterfall.

Eventually, haggard, beyond exhaustion, they staggered into the whaling station at Stromness.

Only once subsequently, 40 years later, in 1955, was South Georgia Island successfully traversed, this time by a British survey team, whose men were expert climbers, fresh, and amply equipped. Their leader wrote of the first crossing: "I do not know how they did it, except that they had to—three men of the heroic age of Antarctic exploration with 50 feet of rope between them—and a carpenter's adze [axe]."[12]

A boat was dispatched to successfully rescue their mates on the other side of South Georgia. But it proved much more difficult to rescue the men on Elephant Island. Within seventy-two hours of arriving at the whaling station, Shackleton was on a ship sailing for Elephant Island. But winter was setting in and thick packs of ice blocked the sea path to their destination. Again and again, in differing ships, Shackleton tried to gain his goal, only to be forced to turn back.... one craft battered by the thick ice through which he tried to push it. Finally, on the fourth attempt, on August 30th, almost four months after Shackleton had sailed on the *James Caird*, they reached Elephant Island and rescued the castaways.

Every one of Shackleton's men survived.

It is one of the most breathtaking survival stories in our history. "Though they had failed dismally even to come close to the expedition's original objective, they knew that somehow they had done much, much more than ever they set out to do."[13]

British scientist and explorer, Raymond Priestley, speaking of polar discoverers, said it best: "For scientific leadership, give me [Robert]

Scott; for swift and efficient travel, [Roald] Amundsen; but when you are in a hopeless situation, when there seems no way out, get on your knees and pray for Ernest Shackleton."

These are nobly uplifting stories, to be sure, worthy of being read, mulled, and savored for their own sake and for many hours.

But, in this context, serious questions emerge: Is it proper to unite these examples into a single classification? If so, by virtue of what? And what about "the folks next door" (everyman and everywoman)? Are these four instances fundamentally different from the so-called "common man"? If so, what makes them different?

We are all human beings, after all. Is there some factual basis for distinguishing these stories from the life stories of other human beings? If so, what is it?

CHAPTER TWO

A Series of Contrasting Stories

From an early age we learn that there are differing kinds of human beings.

We know personally individuals in our family, in our town, at school, and via other venues. By paying attention to current events, by studying history, literature, and other fields, we reinforce our early awareness that individuals are often strikingly diverse from each other; not merely regarding gender, race, nationality, and such matters, but also regarding issues of personal conduct.

For example, some persons will characteristically tell the truth, while others are habitual liars; some will steal our belongings, while others will not, and still others will go to significant lengths to return recovered property that has been stolen from us. Some will bully those smaller and weaker, while others will not, and still others will protect innocent persons from bullies; and so forth.

Those in our immediate purview will be the first about whom we learn; but in not too many years, characters from movies and television shows supplement our understanding; and not long thereafter, they are all joined by characters learned of via current events, history, and literature.

The persons of whom we learn might be real-life or fictitious—and, if real life, personally encountered or not—known perhaps via current events or study of history; these are secondary points. In the present context, what matters is that they provide a basis for comparing and contrasting human beings; for classifying like with like, and of differentiating them from those who are unlike.

As simple illustrations: Let us say (hopefully) that our parents are persons of rectitude, upon whose word we quickly learn we can rely. Further, we learn from history that Abraham Lincoln was famously truthful, known by the nickname of "Honest Abe." Additionally, in literature, when we study Greek mythology, we learn that the god, Apollo, was constitutionally incapable of telling a lie.

All such individuals differ, we note, from sundry liars, cheats, and/ or petty thieves we might meet or learn about, whether in our personal lives, our studies, or via fiction. In such a manner, we form the rudimentary basis of what, later in our cognitive development, will constitute important moral distinctions and classifications.

The basis of the classification "hero" is established via a similar method, by comparing and contrasting differing persons we either encounter personally or whose stories we learn of via current events, history, literature, or through some other medium. Individual human beings are similar regarding certain characteristics and differ regarding others. This point can be made in terms of variables: There are persons who manifest attributes x and who differ from those enacting attributes non-x, where non-x includes a broad range of such differing attributes as y, z, and others.

To discover what some of these attributes are, let us begin with three vivid tales taken from the field of literature, whose portrayals of human beings are starkly different.

Story One

A hard-working, honestly upright man named Eddie works for a transcontinental railroad whose headquarters are in New York. He is

executive assistant to the railroad's vice-president in charge of oper-
ations, his childhood friend, a brilliant young woman named Dagny.
She runs the railroad expertly, builds a branch line superbly, recognizes the value of a controversial new technology immediately, and,
like James J. Hill, Edward H. Harriman, and other great industrialists
of America's past, produces a substantial amount of material wealth.

Eddie, like Dagny, is fully committed to the railroad, to industri-
alization, to the creation of wealth, to increasing living standards, to
escalating prosperity, and to human well-being. But he lacks the ability
to run the railroad and create wealth in the brilliantly effective manner
that Dagny does. He is a conscientious, hard-working, honest employee
but, unlike his boss, he is not a brilliantly productive businessperson.

In the end, as the railroad (and industrial civilization more broadly)
collapses under the weight of repressive government, Eddie journeys to
San Francisco in an attempt to hold the transcontinental line together.
On the train ride back to New York, the locomotive breaks down in
the Arizona desert; Dagny, an accomplished engineer, would be able to
repair it; Eddie, lacking her abilities, is not. It is left ambiguous whether
Eddie, stranded in the desert, perishes, or whether Dagny—a skilled
pilot, possessing a high-powered plane—will be able to rescue him.

Overall, although Eddie cannot run the railroad like Dagny, he is an
honest and valued employee. He has a career, not merely a job, working
productively in a line of work—and for a company—that he loves.

The story of Eddie Willers is a sidebar, a secondary aspect of Ayn
Rand's novel, *Atlas Shrugged*.

Story Two

Eveline, a young woman in Ireland, is in love with a sailor named Frank,
who will take her to Buenos Aires and marry her. Her life in Dublin is
unfulfilling: Her mother had lived an unhappy life, ending in madness
and early death; her father is violent; her favorite brother is dead and

her other, for whom she also cares, is generally away from home for his work; her job as a clerk is unrewarding, and her supervisor treats her badly. Frank, by contrast, is kind and treats her well. She looks forward to her new life in Buenos Aires, although she also remembers her promise to her dying mother to keep the family together as long as she can. Secretly, she has written letters of farewell to her father and her brother.

She meets Frank at the quay. The ship is ready to depart and it is time to board. But a terror seizes her and she grips the railing of the wharf. She refuses to let go, she will not budge. Frank pleads with her to board the ship and go together to their new life. It is her last chance to board, perhaps her final opportunity to change her life. But she will not do it.

"She set her white face to him, passive, like a helpless animal. Her eyes gave him no sign of love or farewell or recognition."

The tale is James Joyce's short story, "Eveline."

Story Three

A Georgia man, Bailey, will take his family—his wife, his son, his daughter, a third child who is a baby, and his mother—on a vacation to Florida. His mother (referred to in the story as "the grandmother") points out that a homicidal maniac calling himself "The Misfit" is loose in Florida and that the family should instead visit relatives in eastern Tennessee. Her son rebuffs her and they drive toward Florida. En route the grandmother repeatedly harangues the family with tales of how much better people were in her day, of what a lady she was, and of the many suitors she had. The children rudely disdain her.

A mistake by the grandmother causes the car to crash in a ditch on an unpaved back road. While the shaken family recovers from the accident, the grandmother flags down a black hearse driving down the road. Three men, armed with guns, emerge. The grandmother says to them that she recognizes the leader as The Misfit, who confirms it. Following The Misfit's orders, his men take Bailey and his son into the woods and shoot them. The shooters return for the mother, the daughter, and the baby to do the same. The grandmother pleads for her own life. She reaches to touch The Misfit's shoulder. He recoils in horror and shoots her three times in the chest, killing her instantly.

When the entire family has been killed, The Misfit says of the grandmother that she would have been a good woman if "it had been somebody there to shoot her every minute of her life." One of his men exclaims "Some fun!" The Misfit replies, "Shut up, Bobby Lee. It's no real pleasure in life."

This tale is Flannery O'Connor's short story, "A Good Man Is Hard To Find."

Assuming we read such stories in our youth, we might yet be too undeveloped, cognitively or morally, to make any sophisticated judgments regarding these characters. We might realize only that: 1. Eddie is an honest, hard-working man who faces the problems confronting him and tries with all of his might to overcome them but, sadly, lacks the ability to do so 2. Eveline is an honest person who wants to change her unhappy situation in life, makes the beginning of an effort to do so, but fails to follow through and, in the end, gives up 3. The Misfit is a murderer, a violent and dangerous man.

Although we may not read these specific stories, they are representative of many similar tales and characters we encounter whether via personal experience, reading, watching television shows or movies, or observing the news.

Contained herein, and in the stories recounted at the outset, is raw material that, when combined with knowledge of many other characters, real or fictitious, lays the foundation for future classifications of differing kinds of human beings—including the classification of "hero."

CHAPTER THREE

What is a Hero?

Most of us, in our personal lives, probably know nobody like either (sadly) Shane or (happily) The Misfit.

But, presumably, we know many who manifest most of the qualities of Eddie Willers. Perhaps our parents, or members of our extended family, or the folks next door, or teachers, or store owners in our town, or so forth, show repeatedly in their actions that they are honest, they work hard and productively, they are responsible, and they can be trusted.

Eddie Willers, and those like him that we know personally, are everyman and everywoman at their best, honest, conscientious, and trustworthy—but not outstanding. They have careers—not merely jobs—often they are happily married, perhaps have children they love, they take parenting seriously, and their lives have both meaning and purpose. But, like Eddie Willers, they lack the prowess to perform some noteworthy deed or create some exalted achievement.

Further, most of us probably know one or two sad instances like Eveline. For example, the man down the street who is in his mid-forties or older, still lives with his parents, and holds a job that, to him, is meaningless. He does not have a career—work that is, to him, deeply meaningful—is not studying in preparation for a future career, is not in a romantic relationship, and has nothing—not the arts, not physical fitness, not reading and learning, nothing—about which he is passionate. His life is lonely and unfulfilled but he is resigned to it.

The Evelines of the world, whether we know them personally or read about them, are harmless lost souls, sweetly hapless, who are referred to (pejoratively) as sad sacks or nebbishes or the like.

Hopefully, we don't know anybody like The Misfit. But stories of violent criminals are, in our purview, inescapable. For example, the news contains stories of many differing kinds of murderers—the trial and conviction of a man who murdered his wife, or of a woman who murdered her children, or of gang violence and multiple cold-blooded killings in many U.S. cities. We see "true crime" stories on television of such serial killers as Ted Bundy (who murdered at least 30 young women), Jeffrey Dahmer (who ate some of his victims), John Wayne Gacy (who buried the remains of 26 of his victims in the crawl space of his home), and others.

Related, the Hollywood film, *Silence of the Lambs*, told the grisly story of several serial killers, including that of Hannibal Lecter, a psychopathic killer who (like Dahmer in real-life) ate some of his victims; the movie and, to a lesser extent, the novel on which it was based, were widely known in popular culture. Finally, innumerable popular movies are produced, featuring gangsters who cold-bloodedly murder anybody who stands in the way of their rise to ill-gotten wealth.

Stories of persons similar to The Misfit are widely known in our society.

Fortunately, although we may not know, in our personal lives, any individuals like Shane (or Montessori, Carver, or Shackleton), here too our cultural awareness is flooded with multiple examples of like characters—of men and women who, in various forms, supplement unusual prowess with notable courage and/or perseverance in benefit to human life.

Consider just a few more examples:

One: In grade school, we study the real-life tale of an intrepid explorer who, in the absence of charts, reliable maps, and the most elementary knowledge of what to expect on the other side of the world, led a 16th century mission that succeeded in circumnavigating the globe, thereby opening, in time, world-wide routes of trade and emigration.

Two: We learn of the great scientist who identified that many serious ailments are caused by microscopic organisms—germs—and how leading thinkers of his day, thinking him mad, bitterly denounced him. His accomplishment, we understand, led to treatments and cures of numerous lethal diseases.

Three: We learn of the black American man born into slavery in Maryland, who struggled against his "owners" to learn to read and write; who escaped from slavery, reaching freedom in the northern states; who developed into a brilliant writer, an eloquent speaker against human slavery, and a leader of America's 19th century Abolitionist movement. He was a principled and uncompromising opponent of the pro-slavery forces in the United States. His accomplishments, we learn, contributed substantially to the ending of slavery in the country.

Starting in childhood and continuing throughout our lives, we are bombarded by a torrent of encounters and stories, revealing a welter of differing characters and their various attributes.

Forming Classifications of Differing Kinds of Human Beings

Most likely we know many hard-working, honest but not outstanding individuals. We might know, or at least hear or read about, several sad cases of good-natured persons who drift aimlessly through life, lacking purpose and passion, finding little or no meaning. Via several media, we are familiar with numerous stories of murderers and other violent criminals. By the same means, we know of those individuals, real or fictitious, who exhibit ability and courage in unusual quantities, deploying these to bring—in various forms—significant gain to human life.

(It is suggested here neither that these four kinds of persons exhaust the range of human types nor that there is an absence of cross-pollination and mixed cases. It is asserted merely that these are four various kinds of human beings with whom we often come in direct contact and/or hear about.)

We observe the similarities and differences that do, in fact, exist.

We notice, for example, that our father, like several of our aunts and uncles, and like the couple next door, hold steady jobs; they rarely miss days of work; they talk seriously about the problems faced and tasks accomplished; they deposit their pay in their checking accounts and spend the preponderance of their money to support their families. Like Eddie Willers, they have a productive career and a meaningful life; unlike Shane, they lack outstanding prowess and/or courage; but, within a circumscribed range, are potent, manifesting none of Eveline's haplessness; and, unlike The Misfit, evince no aggressive violence of even a slight degree, much less lethal.

From such a range of like individuals, contrasted with those significantly unlike, we form the classification of honestly productive persons.

We have met such persons as the fortyish man down the street who lives with his parents, who holds a job to him of little or no meaning, who has no lover or good friend, who has nothing that he passionately loves, and who, sadly, drifts aimlessly through life. We have read stories of such similar cases as Eveline. We see that they differ from Eddie Willers and those like him, who lead a richly fulfilling life; we observe that they differ sharply from The Misfit and similar persons, who are hardened, soulless killers; and we see that they also differ sharply from Shane and those like him, who exhibit noteworthy ability and courage, deployed in promotion of human life.

From instances such as these, and from the contrasting others, we form the classification of harmlessly hapless persons.

We probably know nobody like The Misfit or Ted Bundy or Jeffry Dahmer or one of that ilk but, unfortunately, stories of them are all too common. They differ importantly, we observe, from the honestly productive persons, the sadly hapless persons, and the individuals of grand-scale accomplishments, in that these others manifest a respect for human life, which The Misfits of the world do not.

From such a panoply of bloody examples—and the contrasting others—we form the classification of murderers.

Mixed in this bombardment of personal encounters with, and stories of a broad range of diverse persons, are the tales of those like Shane and all of the others referenced above—Montessori, Carver, and Shackleton, as well as Ferdinand Magellan, Louis Pasteur, and Frederick Douglass. These are individuals who stand out from their brothers and sisters in their ability, in some combination of courage and/or perseverance in the teeth of daunting obstacles, and especially in their commitment to positive, constructive, life-advancing goals, for example, protecting the innocent, exploring the world, making educational or medical advances, and abolishing human slavery.

How do we designate those who enhance human life on a grand scale—especially those who, in order to do so, must face formidable impediment or antagonism?

We need a category for them that is distinct from those of the various other types of persons we encounter or about whom we read.

That category is the classification "hero."

Based on a limited range of particulars, and an expanse of differing examples from which the first range of particulars is distinguished, we form the concept of "hero."

At this point, we have a rough understanding of heroes as persons who perform deeds that, in some form, sustain or improve human life and, in so doing, face down powerful impediments or opposition that would dismay lesser men.

We now have criteria of selectivity. We have seen the method by which this concept is formed—and we have identified several characteristics of heroism.

We have distinguished a handful of human beings embodying these traits from many who do not.

Note the many differences between and among these figures: Six are male, one is female—five are white, two are black—four are European, three are American—six are real-life, one is fictional—one is a gunfighter, one an educator, one a writer/orator, two are scientists, and two are explorers.

Deepening Our Understanding of the Characteristics of a Hero

But these factors are inconsequential. It is the deeper similarities they share that are important.

What are these?

One: Heroes take action in significant promotion of human life. For example, they pioneer innovative educational theories that, when applied in practice, significantly advance cognitive development in early childhood—or they revolutionize agricultural science, teaching mankind how to develop new foodstuffs or more efficiently maintain soil fertility—or they explore remote regions of the earth, increasing human knowledge of our home planet, and bring all their men back alive—and others like them perform many similar life-enhancing deeds.

Two: They are dauntless.

The *American Heritage Dictionary*, Fifth Edition, defines "daunt" as: "To lessen the courage or resolution of; dishearten or intimidate." Its definition of "dauntless" is: "Incapable of being intimidated or discouraged; fearless." There are confusions here—and this issue can be made more precise. One point is: There is a complex of obstacles that heroes might face.

First, there is the inherent difficulty of resolving intractable problems—for example, of discovering new knowledge in education or in agricultural science. Second, there is opposition from powerful forces, be these natural, social (or perhaps internally psychological)—or any combination of these.

It takes *perseverance* to confront and overcome profoundly recondite problems: Thomas Edison, for example, spent years of painstaking effort researching an incandescent electric light; he was tenacious in his pursuit, refusing to relent. He was undeterred by the problem's refractory nature.

It takes *courage* to face powerful forces arrayed against one's aspirations. Shackleton, confronting raging seas, bitter cold, and impassable peaks, faced formidable, potentially lethal natural forces. Montessori and Carver, confronting some combination of social prejudice, racial bigotry, and Fascist regimes, faced perniciously potent social forces.

Perseverance is not the same thing as courage, which the *American Heritage Dictionary* defines as: "The state or quality of mind that enables one to face danger, fear, or vicissitudes with self-possession, confidence, and resolution; bravery."

It definitely takes courage to stand up to opposition from powerful forces; there is danger in crossing Antarctic seas in an open boat, in fighting for liberty against the armies of the world's mightiest empire (George Washington), in defying secular and/or religious authority (Socrates, Galileo, and numerous others).

There is little peril in seeking to advance human knowledge of agricultural science or invent an incandescent electric light bulb. There is immense difficulty in this, not danger to one's life, freedom, or loved ones.

Heroism may lie in facing either or both of these problems.

Most important: Whether heroes confront intractable difficulty, grave danger, or both—whether their achievements involve perseverance, courage, or both—they accept the challenge and face up to the impediment/opposition.

They need not be fearless. But they are dauntless—they are perennially undeterred.

They may be exhausted but they persevere. They may be fearful but they face danger courageously. They may be both exhausted and fearful but they do not quail in the face of obstacle and/or danger.

Heroes are undeterred by profoundly intractable problems and/or by dangerously potent antagonists. In the face of either or both, they are undaunted.

Three: To successfully navigate such obstacles and/or dangers in accomplishment of life-giving goals involves the development and deployment of prowess—whether intellectual, bodily, or an integration of the two—at a level above and beyond that of everyman. These are deeds that the intelligent layman, even at his finest, cannot perform. Navigating turbulent seas and towering peaks in bitter cold requires robust mental and bodily toughness. Discovering new scientific knowledge or revolutionizing elementary education entails intellectual genius. To accomplish difficult and/or dangerous tasks requires a level of capacity equal to the assignment. To successfully complete herculean labors entails herculean prowess.

Four: Such individuals achieve triumph—perhaps in practical terms, perhaps not—but always in a moral sense. They may fall short of their specific goal; they might fail to traverse the Antarctic land mass, for instance; they might even be shot in the back and die—but their dauntless quests are undying in a form their bodies are not. They show us, in action, the human capacity for unbreached dedication to a life-promoting goal.

Their uncowed spirit in the face of extreme difficulty and/or danger remains perennially an inspiration.

We may formulate more succinctly the salient characteristics of heroism:

1. Action in substantial promotion of human life.
2. Dauntlessness in the face of intractable difficulty and/or dangerous opposition.
3. Substantial prowess, above and beyond that of the best of everyman.
4. Victory in at least a moral sense.

Examine these four attributes at a deeper level.

One: Action in significant promotion of human life.

There is an evaluative component in the designation of one as a hero. The appellation signifies more than a factual identification that one's deeds substantially enhanced human life and that they involved application of surpassing ability; there is, in addition, the assessment that to do such is good. The point can be phrased colloquially—a hero is "a good guy."

But good—by what standard?

Human beings often hold, and have long held differing, at times clashing moral principles, codes, and standards. Which one is rationally appropriate?

In the end, each human being must look unprejudicially at the facts of nature and of human life and, employing his/her most conscientiously best rational judgment, determine the matter for himself.

In this writer's judgment, the factual requirements of human life form the proper standard by which to appraise something as good or evil. All that which advances the life of a rational being is good; all that which harms, undermines, or destroys human life is evil. Those who support this standard of right and wrong will accept the definition of heroism that logically follows; those who reject it, will not. (See Appendix A: "Human Life as the Standard of Moral Value.")

A hero, then, is committed to the requirements of human life. A hero places his/her prowess in service of life, not death; of achievement, not destruction; of creativity, not plunder.

Imagine significant prowess—intellectual, bodily, or both—placed not in service of advancing life, but rather, of undermining or expunging it. Suppose, for example, that Maria Montessori had deployed her genius to stunt rather than nurture children's independent thinking— that Douglas MacArthur had put in service to the Axis powers rather than the Americans his commanding leadership qualities—that, to take a fictional example, Sherlock Holmes employed his formidable intellect to foment rather than to foil murder. The results of their actions would be large-scale destruction, not construction; death, rather than life; villainy, not heroism.

There are no evil heroes. Perhaps Hitler or Stalin, had they made differing choices, might have equaled Winston Churchill in statesmanship. But they did not. One toiled prodigiously to protect the freedom of man's mind; the others to enslave it. Consequently, one is a great hero; the others, execrable villains. The phrase "evil genius" might or might not have legitimacy. But the phrase "evil hero" is an oxymoron.

Unprejudicial observation of facts shows a rare but undeniable truth: Certain supremely-gifted individuals use those gifts to immensely facilitate human life.

Two: Dauntlessness in the face of extreme difficulty and/or powerful antagonism.

In pursuit of life-affirming goals, a hero is willing to confront any obstacle or danger impeding his path. He/she is deterred by neither recondite problems nor antagonistic forces that will dishearten a lesser man. Nobody's exploits display this virtue as compellingly as those of Shackleton, already described.

Although courage—as distinct from perseverance—is not necessarily a component of heroism, on numerous occasions it is; for the powerful opposition often faced by a hero calls for and calls forth this virtue. The dictionary definition previously cited is excellent. But an important point, drawn from moral philosophy, must be added; that is, the relationship of courage to the virtue of integrity.

"Integrity" is conventionally defined as the policy of remaining true, in action, to one's principles, convictions, or values. An important amendment here must be made: Having integrity is being true, in action, not simply to any principles one happens to hold, but to *rational, healthy, life-advancing principles*.[14]

For example, Hitler undoubtedly held principles—the existence of a master race, its proper destiny to conquer and rule, the rectitude of enslaving and/or annihilating "racial inferiors," and so on; further, he lived by, and died for such principles. Does this make him a man of integrity? No. Virtues are qualities that promote human life, not ones that expunge it. One of history's most detestable mass murderers holds no moral virtues, integrity or otherwise.

Courage is integrity in a context: A person holds creative, constructive, positive, productive values and/or principles. In some form, these are threatened, or opposed, or assailed—but such an individual protects them, regardless of the danger. Whether it is his/her freedom, family, career, wealth, mind, or life, when values held dear are endangered, he stands tall in their support, whatever the risks incurred. Cyrano, to take a fictional and somewhat hyperbolic example, to defend his dear friend, single-handedly fights one hundred men.

Three: Prowess perhaps superlative, but at least proportionate to the life-giving task to be effectuated.

A towering hero possesses towering capacity, which enables him/her to achieve values at a level beyond that of everyman. Such ability can take differing forms—whether fighting skills, like Shane—or seamanship and leadership abilities, a la Shackleton and Magellan—or intellect, like Montessori, Carver, Douglass and Pasteur. Such capacities underlie and make possible the life-giving accomplishments of these individuals—and enable them to triumph over obstacles and/or antagonism that might dismay one of lesser capacity.

There is a belief in sports: "There is no substitute for talent." If taken literally, the claim is false; for a competitor with lesser skill might—with greater initiative—outhustle and consequently out play a superior talent. Nevertheless, there is a hard nugget of truth contained in the statement: When the wills to compete are generally equal, the greater talent will prevail.

Fortunately for mankind, some standout individuals tower above the best of everyman, and achieve heights unattainable to him. For example, Maurice Hilleman, a researcher at Merck, developed vaccines to effectively inoculate human beings from numerous lethal ailments—becoming the man credited with saving more human lives than any medical scientist of the 20th century[15]—a pinnacle unscalable by any of many conscientious high school biology instructors. Similarly, Steve Jobs (and Stephen Wozniak), not one of the many other dedicated computer hobbyists of the 1970s, founded Apple and went on to revolutionize the computer industry. Illustrations of this principle could be drawn from every field of human endeavor. To reach unparalleled achievement, great talent is as indispensable as great work ethic.

Is great talent made, rather than born? Certainly there exists today the inspiring belief—based on a good deal of research—that roughly 10,000 hours of conscientious practice, over the course of a lifetime, facilitates excellence in a given field.[16] Honest observation of human life tends, to a degree, to provide corroboration. Certainly any number of high achievers, over centuries, in a diverse array of fields, have attained command following the time-honored exhortation: "Practice makes perfect." (If it does not literally make "perfect," it certainly makes mastery.)

But consider the following thought experiment: A conscientious, competent high school physics teacher devotes much of his/her leisure—weekends, holidays, summer vacations, across years and decades—to studying science, reaching—indeed, far surpassing—the recommended 10,000 hours. Is this sufficient to create the equivalent of Newton? It is an error to ignorantly disparage the gifts of a given individual; in this case, perhaps it is.

But what if we replicated the experiment ten thousand times? A hundred thousand? A million? Would the result be ten thousand or one hundred thousand or a million equivalents of Newton? Certainly, such individuals will substantially advance their skills, and expedite increasingly elevated achievement—but sufficient to discover nature's concealed secrets and universal laws?

There are, as yet, no definitive answers to such questions. But it seems unlikely; for presumably, over the years and the ages, many competent persons have put in diligent hours practicing basketball without becoming the equal of Michael Jordan; or investigating philosophy without rivaling Aristotle; or writing creatively without attaining the achievements of Shakespeare; and so forth. A certain talent level, higher than the best of everyman—innate, in-born, biologically hard-wired—is a likely second pre-requisite, in addition to copious amounts of concentrated practice, to attainment of the highest levels of human accomplishment.

From these three characteristics emerge the final heroic attribute.

Four: Victory in at least a moral sense.

A hero achieves victory in some form, moral if not practical. It is possible that an individual of the type described above might fail in his/her specific quest—or die—or be defeated and/or murdered by his enemies; but his/her undaunted and unbreached dedication to values represents, at the very least, a moral triumph.

Cyrano constitutes an impeccable fictional example; for none of his specific values are attained. His brilliant plays are not performed; his deep, soul-consuming love for Roxane is not consummated; and he is ambushed and treacherously killed by cowardly, perfidious foes. And yet, his principled independence that will not truckle to authority, his unbending integrity that refuses to betray his soul, his unyielding allegiance to what he knows is right, and his fearless willingness to face all enemies—these are deathless qualities that perennially inspire readers to seek the best within themselves.

The essence of "hero" is an undaunted and supremely able commitment to life-enhancing values in the teeth of extreme difficulty and/or opposition. The rare human being who achieves this qualifies as a hero, regardless if, sadly, he/she fails or dies in his specific attempt.

If, for example, George Washington, after overcoming seemingly insurmountable obstacles to keep alive military resistance in support of American freedom, had died before final victory at Yorktown, his status as hero would perhaps be diminished but not nullified—similarly, even if massive British reinforcements had ultimately quashed the rebellion.

To scale the highest levels of human achievement, practical success is preferred but not required. There are greater or lesser heroes, as ranked in terms of ordinal numbers—and since successful living is the ultimate goal, practical triumph is one criterion of heroism. But it is by no means the sole one; and even in noble failure, an individual of the kind under discussion furthers human life, whether via practical victories he/she scores before his demise and/or by inspiration he provides other persons to sustain lofty struggles of their own.

At the very least, a hero shows, in action, the stature potentially attainable by human beings.

Our Need of Heroes

Why, then, do human beings require heroes?

For two reasons.

The first is practical. Often, tasks profoundly supportive of human life are arduous, at times dangerous. Socrates, for example, provided both method and content to catalyze the nascent field of moral philosophy, an intellectual feat both difficult and beneficial in the extreme; and, achieving controversy equal to his stature, faced execution as a result.

Maria Montessori, in similar fashion, revolutionized elementary education, an attainment likewise entailing commanding intellect. In teaching children to think, to follow their autonomous judgment rather than the state, she predictably incurred the hostility of Italy's Fascist regime. But, fortunately, rather than execution, she suffered state surveillance, closure of her Italian schools, and estrangement from her homeland.

To face such challenges, to overcome intractable impediments and/ or dangers, to persevere in their presence, to courageously confront, to uphold, to withstand, to triumph—such feats require individuals of singular ability and of dauntless makeup.

In practical terms, heroes place mankind on their supportive shoulders and carry human beings into flourishing civilization.

Second and not to be under-valued is a hero's inspirational role in human life. For many persons facing hardship or handicap, dauntlessness is augmented by recollection of severe tribulations unflinchingly and triumphantly faced by a Shackleton or another such hero.

Such an inspirational role model may be especially important when young, a theme Jack Schaefer dramatizes brilliantly, poignantly in his novel. But often overlooked is a hero's similar internal benefit in the lives of adults.

One wonders, for example, about the positive impact wrought by the events of Apollo 13 in April, 1970. After the spacecraft suffered a mission-crippling explosion on approaching the moon, a lunar landing became impossible. Calmly, Jim Lovell, space veteran and mission commander, uttered the oft-repeated (if slightly mangled) words: "Houston, we've had a problem."

There was legitimate question that the astronauts could survive the journey back to Earth. But via generous portions of courage, scientific genius, and engineering expertise, the astronauts and Mission Control in Houston were able to navigate the vessel safely home.

Millions of people watched the great survival drama unfold on TV. The courage, the expertise, the preternatural calm of the astronauts— did these grand-scale qualities go unnoticed and unadmired? One would guess they did not.

Were some, perhaps many, motivated by such a sight of human stature to feel or even think: If these few men can overcome explosion in space and a damaged vessel to traverse vast distances back to Earth, I, who face obstacles in my path neither as dismaying nor as lethal, what might I accomplish? Presumably, the answer to this question is a resounding yes.

A hero might never know who, and how many, he/she psychologically and morally uplifts.

"The sight of an achievement was the greatest gift a human being could offer to others," heroine Dagny Taggart reflects in Ayn Rand's *Atlas Shrugged*.

Why? Because if one individual, within the scale of his/her interests and abilities, overcomes impediments and achieves at a high level, then another human being—member of the same species with the same fundamental attributes—by enacting the requisite causation, can likewise, within the scale of his/her abilities and concerns, also achieve at an appropriately high level.

Heroes show, in action, that human stature is more than mere theory.

As Shane with Bobby, this is the psychological/moral value offered by heroes to those who want to live.

A Definition of Hero

What, then, is a hero?

Admiral James Stockdale, in his 1991 lecture, "On Heroes and Heroism," stated: "Let me tell you they are out there—those of confounding selflessness and seeming immunity to fear.... They have eluded concise definition since the beginning of recorded history."[17]

Peter Gibbon, in his book, *A Call To Heroism*, affirms Stockdale's claim. He writes: "The moral component of the meaning of heroism— and, I believe, the most important one—is elusive."[18]

Although Gibbon's book is insightful and inspiring, he acknowledges that he can arrive at no definition of "hero." He states: "The definition of *hero* remains subjective. What is extraordinary can be debated. Courage is in the eye of the beholder. Greatness of soul is elusive."[19]

Philosopher, Sidney Hook, in his book, *The Hero In History*, seeks to understand history in terms of the impactful causal agents who shape its events. Toward this end, he distinguishes between what he calls "the eventful man" and "the event-making man." An eventful man, he says, is one whose actions direct historic occurrences along paths they would not otherwise have taken in the absence of those actions. An event-making man, he continues, is an eventful man who takes the momentous actions he does not merely because of luck, happenstance, or favorable circumstances but by virtue of wisdom, courage, and/or strength of character. "This distinction tries to do justice to the general belief that a hero is great not merely in virtue of what he does but in virtue of what he is."[20] Nevertheless, Professor Hook does not provide a rigorous definition of the concept.

But since heroes are real, as illustrated by the above discussion, they are something. They manifest a definite and, therefore, identifiable set of characteristics and eschew others. Put simply, they are what they are.

We have already seen what they are.

Heroes are dedicated to promoting human life. They may or may not be consistent, but to the extent that they are heroic—in the deeds that make them heroes—they take action in support of human well-being.

The genus of the concept "hero" is the broad class of ethically upright persons, meaning those who act to advance human life. Heroes form a sub-category of the class of good guys.

What separates heroes from more pedestrian good guys is their prowess and their dauntlessness. They manifest both greater ability than their commonplace brethren and an attitude less dismayed by adversity. This enables them to enact life-advancing deeds on an epic scale.

It might be argued that heroes arise in contexts of crisis: Winston Churchill, after-all, ascended to greatness in the death struggle of World War II; Socrates in the confrontation with authority regarding the morally proper way to deploy great power; Frederick Douglass amidst the moral contradiction resulting from the existence of human slavery in a republic founded upon the principle of each individual's inalienable right to liberty.

This is undoubtedly true. But if heroes arise during periods of baleful tumult, then, sadly, they lack no historic opportunity. Virtually every era has its equivalent of slavery or Hitler or massive outbreak of lethal disease; no human epoch lacks for catastrophe and/or atrocity.

But heroes, with significant prowess and unsurpassed dauntlessness, transform calamity into opportunity; willing themselves to face dangerous impediment, to take amelioratory action, and to thereby promote human life.

Long ago, Socrates understood the importance of forming precise definitions of moral concepts. The current writer possesses neither Socrates' genius nor his courage—but, by forming a precise definition of the elusive concept of "hero," sustains the great philosopher's enterprise.

It may be that we will amend the following definition of "hero" later when we examine the possibility that the moral best of everyman, in some sense, might achieve the status of "hero."

But it was most likely by reference to giants—examples of whom have been discussed here—that mankind originally formed the concept of "hero." The good guys most efficacious and undismayed in facilitating life-promoting goals were those who most elevated themselves above the group of their everyday brethren—who stood out—and who, consequently, were those first singled out and designated as "heroes." We have sufficient information to formulate a rough, working definition of "hero."

A hero is: *A morally upright individual who, with ability and dauntlessness exceeding that of everyman, confronts the obstacles and/ or dangers arising in pursuit of significant life-advancing goals, and who triumphs in at least a moral sense.*

CHAPTER FOUR

Everyman a Hero?

So far, this book has discussed instances of exalted heroes—men and women of both superlative prowess and dauntless makeup who overcame intractable obstacles and/or dangers to reach accomplishments that substantially enhanced human life.

The book has examined heroes of epic proportion.

But what of noble souls who, perhaps, lack the capacity of a George Washington Carver, of a Maria Montessori, of an Ernest Shackleton? Are they not often men and women of notable perseverance and/or courage? Do not the moral best of everyman, at times, engage in demanding struggles to support life—and, in some percentage of such cases, emerge victorious?

Examples of Everyman and Everywoman Performing Heroic Deeds

Consider an airline pilot, for example, who, upon suddenly losing power in both engines shortly after take-off, fights to retain control of the aircraft, glides it, and achieves safe landing in a nearby river, saving thereby the lives of every individual on board.

Take the case of a poor black woman in the Jim Crow-era American South, a sharecropper, who battles bigotry, legalized segregation, and racially-driven violence to rear her children with love, guidance, moral training, and an excellent education, providing them an opportunity extremely difficult to dream of, much less attain, under such arduous conditions.

A battered wife, fearful for her life, rounds up her children, packs them in the family SUV, secretly moves three states away, and quietly starts a new life, perhaps working multiple jobs to independently support herself and the children.

Further, we can think of anonymous firefighters, who risk their lives to save persons, to them, utter strangers.

Aren't there numerous instances of such "ordinary" men and women who, on occasion, rise to extraordinary levels of bravery and/ or accomplishment?

Some of the above tales are fictitious, some are true to life, but all are possible; and the imaginative ones share important characteristics with real-life stories of individuals performing similarly notable deeds.

Such actions certainly appear heroic. So is it not understandable if the passengers, the children, the residents hold up as heroes the pilot, the mother, the firemen? Often, honest persons will say that so-and-so is "my hero." Is not this more than mere figure of speech? In such cases as the above, such an appraisal would appear warranted by the facts.

Life's Daunting Challenges

Every honest person faces challenges in life, including, for example, some of the following: illness and/or extreme pain, death of loved ones, romantic heartbreak, social prejudice, racial bigotry, business failure and/or bankruptcy, and for all, awareness of mortality and the grim certainty of eventual death.

Some individuals face the painful events with sublime courage.

Everyman or everywoman, in numerous forms and instances, seeks positive, life-enhancing values—is confronted by potent impediments and/or opposition—refuses to sacrifice his/her goals—proceeds to struggle vigorously to the utmost of capacity—and, in numerous cases, overcomes obstacles and carries an arduous quest to successful resolution.

Such actions are indubitably heroic.

Hero to a Specific Degree

There might be individuals of great courage and/or perseverance but lesser talent than the grand-scale heroes we have discussed. Such persons might dauntlessly face significant dangers and obstacles, effectuate life-enhancing results, but do so on a scale less expansive than their more talented peers.

For example, take the case of a steadfast assistant to a brilliant medical researcher, without whom the developed cures and/or treatments could not have been properly effected.

The researcher, conceiving seminal insights, is responsible for the preponderance of advance; but the assistant, providing supportive aid, contributes substantially to the outcome. Is not he/she also a hero, although perhaps of lesser stature?

Are there degrees of heroism?

To take a sports analogy, in Major League Baseball's Hall of Fame there are memorialized a number of giants—Babe Ruth, Willie Mays, Ted Williams, Joe Dimaggio, Hank Aaron, Lou Gehrig, Sandy Koufax, among others—and alongside them, a number of players that, while excellent, are not among the sport's immortals—Paul Molitor, Robin Yount, and Don Sutton, as well as others, come to mind. It is possible to attain exceptional expertise in a field without commanding it as an all-time great.

As there are degrees of elevated stature in human life, so there may be degrees of heroism. Ayn Rand, writing of the complex philosophic issue of concept-formation, identified the salient principle: The human mind integrates existents in accordance with characteristic(s) shared in common, *although those characteristics often differ in quantity.* A housecat and a lion, for example, are both cats, possessing the same biologic characteristics but differing in quantity—size, strength, speed, and so forth.

Rand's principle can be applied to assessing Major League Baseball Hall-of-Famers—take position players, for example. They have commonly-shared characteristics—they all have some number of base hits, home runs, runs scored, runs driven in, and so forth. But they have differing amounts of these achievements. Giants such as Ruth, Aaron, and Mays, for example, hit many more home runs than most Hall-of-Famers. All of the position players commemorated in Cooperstown hold commonly-shared characteristics that are of measurable degree and that vary in quantity.

As there are superb baseball players of greater and lesser degree, so there are heroes of greater and lesser degree.

Take two examples: The Jim Crow-era black mother, mentioned above, who secured an excellent education for her children—and Booker T. Washington, who both ran Tuskegee Institute and also helped found throughout the legally-segregated South *thousands of schools* to educate black children.

What are the similarities between them? What are the difference(s)?

Via unstinting devotion to education, a profound human value, each manifested abundant virtue; each combated powerful forces and overcame daunting racist obstacles; both achieved triumph not merely in a moral, but in a practical form, as well. To accomplish arduous tasks both exhibited generous portions of undaunted character—and of ability to differing degrees.

Notice that the extent, the scope, the degree, the amount, *the quantity* of achievement dramatically varies. The anonymous mother's accomplishment, while admirably noteworthy, is on a modest scale; Washington's on a vastly grander one. When we omit the scale, *the measurements,* are both heroes? Washington, without a doubt; the mother—in the judgment of this author, yes.

When we re-introduce the specific measurements, we see not merely that the scope of attainment differs, but the probable cause, as well—their varying degrees of prowess: Washington was brilliant, a mind with power to think on a broad scale and to plan long-range; the mother, presumably highly intelligent but lacking Washington's genius.

Each is a hero but, within this noble category, represents differing degrees of stature: Although both attain elevated heights, one towers above the other. One is a greater, the other a lesser hero.

Recall in this regard that writers of classical mythology distinguished between gods and demigods, the latter defined as either half-divine and half-human or, more appropriate in this context, as lesser deities. Such nomenclature is useful regarding this issue: It might be effective to distinguish between heroes and *demi-heroes,* the latter understood as unequivocally heroic but secondary to their more accomplished peers.

There exist between heroes and demi-heroes a significant difference of degree; a divergence in the measure of prowess that leads inexorably to difference regarding the measure of life-enhancing outcomes.

Everyman at his best, *in any field,* lacks the capacity of a Winston Churchill in statesmanship, of a Duke Ellington in musical composition, of a Maurice Hilleman in medical research, of an Amelia Earhart in aviation, of a Ben Carson in neurosurgery.

There is an observable reality basis for a distinction between mankind's very good and mankind's best. Presumably, by 1939, for example, any number of upright Britons recognized the threat posed by Hitler, and desired victory over National Socialism, but could any of them have led Britain as brilliantly and effectively as did Churchill?

Or, to alter calamitous occurrences, imagine an ebola epidemic (or virus of some terrifyingly similar malignance) sweeps through a nation, infecting thousands or more good persons. Many conscientious medical professionals will, with exceptional courage and to the best of their abilities, combat the disease; some, no doubt, will lose their lives.

Their commitment to human life, their bravery, and their moral stature are not to be doubted—but their capacity to learn to cure or treat the ailment may prove insufficient. Hopefully, there emerges at least one rare individual that manifests an identical degree of devotion, adding to it a towering level of prowess—a degree of ability worthy of Louis Pasteur or Jonas Salk or Maurice Hilleman—that enables him/her to cure or effectively treat the ailment, saving thereby countless human lives.

All of these dauntless physicians and medical researchers have a home in mankind's pantheon of heroes, but within, occupy contrasting rungs of elevation.

Hero in a Delimited Respect

Demi-heroes may be thought of as heroes in a less expansive respect.

In pursuit of specific, healthy, life-advancing goals, they prove indomitable. They may not revolutionize an entire field of human endeavor, as did George Washington Carver and Maria Montessori. But they can and do ameliorate their own lives—and often those within their immediate purview.

In addition to such possible obstacles as painful mourning, divorces and romantic breakups, mindless social prejudices, racism, and the stern reality of death, any person's life, regardless how capable and accomplished, is filled with mundane tasks, perhaps afflicted with nagging ailments, at times plagued with persons troublesomely irrational.

Most persons, for example, perform such deeds as buying food, preparing dinner, and clearing away the untidy result; many suffer from sinus infections, backache, and other annoying maladies; they remonstrate with loud neighbors, quarrelsome family members, and/or squabbling colleagues. Even those who pay servants or assistants to perform pedestrian tasks must instruct and supervise their employees.

And, of course, all honest persons are faced with the sometimes onerous tasks of earning a living and paying their bills.

It is easy to become bogged in life's burdensome chores, to get lost in tangled underbrush and myriad trees, to lose sight of the forest, to drop one's purpose, to relinquish one's struggle, to abandon one's potential.

But these are not necessarily preordained outcomes. Sadly, some might succumb in this manner. But others persevere. Either way, this is a choice individuals make.

Egalitarianism—the principle that human beings are or should be generally equal—is, applied to native capacity, manifestly false. Einstein was born with a greater degree of brainpower than everyman; Ben Carson with a rare combination of superb intelligence and "gifted hands" that exceed the best of most persons; Michael Jordan with a peerless set of athletic skills; and so forth.

But egalitarianism is potentially true in the field of applied volition.

In the midst of travail, onerous hardship, and/or interminable mundanities, some individuals, though lacking the intellectual and/or bodily prowess of an epic hero, choose to forge a purpose positive and meaning-laden, maintain it foremost in their vision, struggle to remain actively engaged, and sustain to successful resolution their cause, regardless how arduous its performance.

They do not merely dream of completing college, for example, or of gaining a martial arts black belt, or of starting a business, or of becoming a physician, or of performing some other demanding task. They do more than wish or fantasize: They initiate action, they willingly encounter every roadblock, they strive persistently to prevail, and, in many cases, they succeed. A determined woman who carries to term a very difficult, even life-threatening pregnancy and gives birth is a prime example.

This is what it means to be a hero in a delimited respect: Within the scale of his/her concerns and abilities—in pursuit of positive goals—everyman, at times, will, with undaunted spirit, face opposition, even life-imperiling danger—and refuse to surrender.

To be human is to possess heroic potential.

A particularly striking example is that of a person stricken with a serious, perhaps terminal ailment, who, in service of life, valiantly battles the disease.

Ellen McDonald, a British woman who, early in the 21st century, celebrated her 100th birthday, is a case in point; somebody who beat cancer not once but five times. In the early 1950s, she suffered from breast cancer and had a double mastectomy. Ten years later, she had cancer in the gall bladder, and had it removed. In 1963, she had cancer of the bowel and was not expected to survive. A priest gave her last rites—48 years before she celebrated her 100th birthday in 2011. "I'm a fighter," she told the priest. In her fifth bout with cancer, she underwent a hysterectomy. She said she made it through, in part, "because of my spirit."[21]

In respect of a will to live and of bravery in the face of likely death, Ellen McDonald is a hero.

Elevated dauntlessness is neither guaranteed in individuals of elevated prowess—nor is it reserved exclusively for them. This highly admirable heroic characteristic is fully egalitarian.

Differing Measures of Heroes?

Epic heroes exceed in prowess such delimited heroes but not necessarily in dauntlessness.

Are there differing measures of a hero's stature?

The aforementioned mother, for example, although lacking Booker T. Washington's genius, may face more demanding challenges and/or pronounced dangers than did he. It is certainly possible that the challenges and dangers might tax her capacities more than those faced by Washington did his. Perhaps she must push herself harder to reach her goals than must the epic hero to reach his. Perhaps she must dig deeper, manifest greater inner fortitude, summon higher levels of courage to fulfill her quest, and so forth.

Prowess and magnitude of achievement are but two criteria of a hero's stature. There are others.

By measure of difficulties and dangers confronted relative to a hero's ability, and by the degree of courage required to face these, it is certainly possible that a smaller-scale achiever might be more heroic than a grand-scale one.

When we study heroes of more modest ability, an important truth emerges: Heroism is largely a moral concept. Regardless the degree of capacity possessed, a hero places it consistently in service of life-promoting goals. A more exact definition of heroes, based on a sample wider than those few of majestic proportion, will de-emphasize prowess in favor of character as heroism's most salient trait. Lawrence Reed makes this important point succinctly: "If I had to pick one point above all others as essential to heroism it would be this: *character*."[22]

An amended definition of a hero is: *A morally upright individual who, with ability and dauntlessness equal to the task, confronts the obstacles and/or dangers arising in pursuit of significant life-advancing goals, and who triumphs in at least a moral sense.*

If human life is the standard of moral value, then magnitude of achievement in promotion of it is one legitimate criterion of heroism. But we must keep in mind that it is not the only one.

CHAPTER FIVE

Morally Flawed Heroes

There may be rare individuals who are heroes throughout the course of their lives—who overcome dismaying obstacles to attain noteworthy goals, and who also display unblemished character in every of life's arenas. They are hard-working students, productive workers, honest friends, attentive spouses, loving parents, and morally upright human beings in every facet of their existences.

But many heroes, perhaps most, whether on a scale epic or less grand, are heroic in respect of a specific project completed or goal attained. The rest of their lives are often mundane or, in some form, tarnished. Shackleton was such an epic hero, who attained one virtually unbelievable goal, and who reached other, less exalted Antarctic triumphs, but the rest of whose life was relatively undistinguished, and whose heavy drinking and smoking most likely contributed to an untimely demise at age forty-seven.

But what about heroes whose lives often include not merely the pedestrian or the less-than-exemplary but the egregiously immoral?

We have examined epic heroes and everyman as hero. But what about morally-flawed heroes? How will rational human beings assess the flagrant moral breaches manifested by some heroes?

This is a complex issue that is best broken down into component parts.

Acts of Abstraction

First, an honest man performs an act of abstraction on a large scale: He/she observes many characteristics of a specific hero—some good, some bad, some indifferent—acknowledges, without denial, the existence of all—but selectively focuses on: The hero's undismayed, effective dedication to life-supporting values in the face of formidable opposition and/or danger.

The honest observer recognizes but holds in abeyance the hero's (or heroine's) specific gender, his/her race or religion, the country or continent of origin, the era in which lived, and other subordinate data.

Second, is the centrally important issue of a proper attitude toward a hero's moral flaws. If such exist, if they are documented and not unsubstantiated accusations hurled by modernist anti-hero mentalities, a rational individual looks reality in the face, recognizes the hero's moral breach(es), acknowledges the ugly truth, deplores it, and proceeds to relegate it to secondary status in his/her assessment. He faces the moral stain, he does not evade or deny it—but recognizes that this is not the most significant truth regarding a hero's life.

Because moral perfection entails neither omniscience nor infallibility, merely stringent commitment to untainted personal responsibility, tireless work ethic, and characteristic truthfulness, it is arduously difficult but possible to attain; indeed, there may well be exalted individuals of impenetrable probity who have done so.

But an absence of moral perfection need not disqualify a prodigious achiever from entree into the pantheon of heroes.

"Heroes sometimes have moral flaws. For example, an individual may spend years of scrupulous, exhausting effort and discover a cure for cancer—and at the same time be unfaithful to his/her spouse. Human beings are not always flawlessly consistent. The point—in justice— is not that the heroic achievement mitigates the moral breach—it does not; rather, it is that the moral breach does not diminish the heroic achievement. In such a case, the injustice committed to the spouse and the glorious attainment are actual occurrences; each is part of reality. Although the dishonesty is to be censured, the supreme accomplishment—and the sedulous devotion to its realization—are to be celebrated."[23]

Excellence and perfection are related but distinct qualities, including in the moral sphere. Ethical failings, even severe ones, where and when substantial virtue and supreme accomplishment obtain as offsetting positives, are not necessarily sufficient to exempt one from the status of hero. Human beings, including great ones, are often morally mixed.

Thomas Jefferson, in both his flaws and his merits, provides a vividly grand-scale illustration of this principle.

Thomas Jefferson as a Morally Flawed Hero

On the negative side, he was a prime player in the vicious political party wars of the 1790s, deliberately spreading demonstrably false rumors about upright men among his Federalist foes: He claimed, for example, that President Washington was, in effect, senile, and several years later that President Adams sought war with France. While Vice-President, he hired a scandalmonger to write a venomous screed against the President, his long-time friend and revolutionary ally, John Adams. He perpetrated such calumnies while vigorously denying culpability, conducting, in the vivid phrase of historian, Joseph Ellis, an "artful minuet with duplicity."[24]

Regarding race relations, he held that blacks were akin to children and racially inferior to whites. As he progressed in age, he regressed in his principled commitment to abolitionism. Despite his genius and like so many of his peers, he could not even envision a bi-racial society.

In addition to all this, is the probable romantic relationship with a slave woman, Sally Hemings, whom, even at his death, he did not free.

Although a theoretical supporter of abolitionism, he "owned" human slaves his entire adult life.

This is not the stuff of which heroes are made.

And yet, the positive side of his ledger displays accomplishments vastly exceeding the merely memorable.

To cite but a few: He was an early and committed supporter of American independence from Great Britain, and, in such undertaking, risked his life. An outstanding prose stylist, he was lead author of *The Declaration of Independence*. He was an unwavering supporter of individual liberties, who adamantly insisted that the Constitution of the fledgling republic be augmented by addition of a Bill of Rights. He strenuously championed religious freedom.

He wrote into the *Declaration of Independence* a passage calling for abolition of the slave trade, which was stricken out by Congress. In the Ordinance of 1784, he called for an end to slavery—by no later than 1800—in the new states to emerge from the Northwest Territories, a clause that failed to pass Congress by a single vote. As President in 1808, he signed into law Congress's resolution to ban the slave trade. Throughout the entirety of his long life, he theoretically favored emancipation of slaves, slowly, by degree, in a cautious method that would not plunge the nascent republic into the horrors and potentially seismic sundering of civil war ... a bloodbath that he accurately foresaw.

Philosophically, he championed the cause of the freethinking human mind, famously "swearing eternal hostility to every form of tyranny over the mind of man." In support of intellectual freedom, he both founded the University of Virginia and donated his massive personal book collection to establish the Library of Congress.

Scientifically, Jefferson pioneered the field of meteorology in the fledgling republic; indeed, was the premier American meteorologist of his time; and his *Notes on the State of Virginia*, for all of its flaws, constituted a milestone in the study of American geography.[25]

Taken together, these diverse characteristics represent a bewildering farrago of discordant elements. How to rationally assess it?

That the man's actions often exhibited significant moral flaws, there can be no doubt. But what degree of moral turpitude is tolerable in a prodigious achiever before dismissal from the echelon of heroes becomes incumbent?

The sad truth is that heroes are sometimes dishonest—and, at times, despite prodigious genius and oft-displayed autonomy of cognitive functioning, on some issues, unconscionably and unforgivably permit themselves to be sucked into the maelstrom of centuries-old, conventional prejudices.

Nevertheless, *The Declaration of Independence*, the Virginia Statute of Religious Freedom, the strenuous support of a Bill of Rights, and the founding of the University of Virginia are life-giving accomplishments of majestic proportion. The first of these, as integral component of his principled commitment to American liberty, placed in grave danger, were he captured, conspicuously more than his income, his estate, or his honor.

In effect, Jefferson's "artful minuet with duplicity" and his racist assumptions, although reprehensible, represent a life parallel to these liberty-promoting achievements, insufficiently commingled to vitiate them.

Related, many individuals are dishonest, even egregiously so, at some point in their lives. But only a rare handful compose *The Declaration of Independence, or* cure virulent ailments, or revolutionize children's education or agricultural science, or reach some similar, surpassing achievement. The infrequency of such accomplishments bears, in itself, testimony to the degree of difficulty involved.

The singularity of such attainment is why Jefferson is distinguished from among a broad range of historic liars, bigots, and slave owners; why he is remembered and they are not; what is of momentous import regarding him, isolated from the mundane, the prosaic, the commonly shared, and the vile; what is outstanding about and unique to him.

Perhaps it is advisable to bifurcate the life of such a supreme achiever as Jefferson (and others) into its noble and ignoble elements;

concluding that, while significant portions are debased and eminently unworthy of a hero, an even more generous segment displays life-giving attainments of grand-scale dimension.

When all factual data are surveyed, and none denied, a rational assessment concludes that Jefferson, to the extent that he manifested the exalted attainments described above, is a towering hero in the historic cause of personal liberty; emphatically not a hero insofar as he perpetrated the aforementioned ethical transgressions. To echo Aristotle's carefully-reasoned mode of formulation: Jefferson is a hero when considered in one respect but not in the other.

Thomas Jefferson is a significantly flawed hero—but a hero, he indubitably is.

This considered judgment regarding such a deeply-flawed hero as Jefferson, an authentic attempt at objectivity, at justice, illustrates the process of rigorous assessment undertaken by a rational individual; certainly, it demonstrates the type of objective judgment that an admirer of heroes might and ought to make.

As such, Jefferson's story affords an ideal test case of how rational hero admirers properly appraise morally-delinquent heroes.

After acknowledging and condemning a hero's actual flaws, a rational admirer of heroes *abstracts away from them*. By a mental process of selective attention, he/she focuses on a small subset of qualities: Life-giving achievement, dedication to an ideal that made it possible, difficulties and/or dangers courageously faced, and superlative prowess enabling successful resolution.

What justifies such an act of abstraction?

The Good Properly Outweighs the Evil

Recognition that what advances human life, what makes life possible— not that which wounds or retards it—is and ought to be of first importance to a rational individual.

The evil is the irrational, the mindless, the aggressively violent, the willfully destructive in body or spirit. Such evil—whether it be a criminal, a dictator, a religious zealot slaughtering innocents, a teacher or clergyman seeking control of the mind, or others—is to be recognized, exposed, denounced, opposed, defeated; then, although never forgotten, held in abeyance. Vigilance against evil is a virtue. Granting it pre-eminence in one's life is not.

But the good—whether a writer or musician composing a great novel or symphony, a scientist advancing human knowledge, an entrepreneur inventing and manufacturing new technologies, a teacher nurturing intellectual growth, a loving parent, a loyal friend, and so forth—is to be celebrated, upheld, rewarded, embraced.

Leonard Peikoff makes this point effectively: "Justice consists first not in condemning, but in admiring.... It consists first in acknowledging the good.... Evil must be combatted, but then it is to be brushed aside. What counts in life are the men who support life. They are the men who struggle unremittingly, often heroically, to achieve values. They are the Atlases whom mankind needs desperately, and who in turn desperately need the recognition—specifically, the moral recognition—to which they are entitled.... It is important to tell Kant that he has rejected reality and is wrong; it is more important that Aristotle find someone who understands that he has recognized reality and is right."[26]

The point can be stated hypothetically: If one chooses to live, then the good must be granted decisive prominence in one's life. The reason: Because the good—neither the wicked nor the morally indifferent—is the characteristic making possible prospering human life.

Put in other terms, a hero to a hero worshiper is like an esthetic work to a Romantic artist: He/she stylizes his conception—he omits or downplays many factually accurate but secondary characteristics in order that he might emphasize the most salient points. Jack Schaefer, for example, glosses over many significant but secondary characteristics of his main character to emphasize but two: Shane's staggering physical prowess, and his undying love for the Starrett family.

By a similar process of abstraction, an honest hero admirer selectively focuses on a hero's prodigious ability to support human life, and recognizes, in Jefferson's case, that in several respects, he is an exalted hero.

Conclusion

Heroes have more than inspirational value to rational individuals. There exists in their actions a cognitive lesson. In a world that may be filled with drudgery and the mundane—or, vastly worse, with numbing violence and callous disregard for human life—heroes show, in action, at a level directly observable, the human potential.

A hero's life-advancing deeds—especially when, like Jefferson's, they are of epic proportion—are akin to a great work of literary art. They form a story worth experiencing, contemplating, savoring, because such a tale offers a vivid, conceptual, at all times visual reminder—it shows us, it does not tell—that human beings can create and effectively protect healthy, prospering enclaves of civilized life.

A hero's life—in the elements of it distinctively heroic—concretizes the moral and metaphysical abstractions that man can be good, and that the good can triumph.

Man, the rational animal, as Aristotle long ago noted, can be rational, not merely an animal.

Heroes, to a hero admirer, serve as a directly experiential embodiment of this truth.

CHAPTER SIX

Heroism as Unbreached Loyalty to Values

The issue of values, and the role they play in human life, forms part of a full understanding of heroism.

A comprehension of the term "value" is implicit in the preceding chapters. It is time to make it explicit—and it is possible to begin with a true story.

A Heroic Life

Teenaged Amelia Earhart, attending a stunt flying exhibition around the time of World War I, stood her ground as a daredevil pilot buzzed both her and her friend. "I did not understand it at the time," she later acknowledged. "But I believe that little red airplane said something to me as it swished by."[27] Few women at the time were aviators, but several years later she took her first ride in a plane. "By the time I had got two or three hundred feet off the ground, I knew I had to fly,"[28] she said.

She was not one to let social prejudices or other obstacles stop her.

Working as a nurse's aide and later as a social worker, she earned enough money to buy her first airplane, which was painted a vivid yellow, and which she dubbed "The Canary." But jesting aside, this canary, like its owner, could fly. Amelia used it to set her first woman's altitude record of 14,000 feet.

This was only the first of many firsts. In May, 1932, five years after the epic flight of Charles Lindbergh, she became the first woman and only the second pilot to fly solo across the Atlantic. She also became the first pilot to fly solo from Hawaii to California; the same from Mexico City to the New York area.

In 1937, nearing her 40th birthday, she attempted to become the first woman pilot to fly around the world. With her navigator, Fred Noonan, she succeeded in traversing 22,000 of the 29,000 mile flight; then, on the morning of July 3rd, searching for her island landing field in cloudy weather over the Pacific Ocean, and her plane running low on fuel, she disappeared. Despite a massive ensuing search, no remains were ever found.[29]

Amelia Earhart lived and died doing what she loved.

Before a dangerous flight, she had written in a letter to her husband: "Please know I am quite aware of the hazards. *I want to do it because I want to do it.* Women must try to do things as men have tried. When they fail this failure must be but a challenge to others."[30] (Emphasis added.)

Amelia Earhart broke ground both as an aviator and as a woman pioneer showing how much was possible. She reached notable achievements because she permitted neither dangerous impediments nor social prejudices to stop her from doing what she loved.

"Never interrupt someone doing something you said couldn't be done,"[31] she stated.

Implicit in her life was the further assertion: "Never interrupt someone doing what they love."

This is what it looks like to hold values, to live in accordance with them, and, if necessary, to die doing that which brings meaning into your life.

Such an inviolable commitment to values is essential to heroism.

The Nature of Values

What are values?

Stated simply, an individual's values are those things, activities, or persons he/she considers of great worth—that which he esteems, prizes, regards as valuable.

An individual might value education, or career in a specific field, or a particular man or woman, or children, or any and all of the above, or one of numerous other possibilities—but whatever his/her values, these are the things, persons, or activities he considers most important in life.

It is often said that actions speak louder than words. The claim is true—and preeminently so regarding values.

An individual might esteem education, as evidenced by hours of study and mastery attained—or career in a specific field, as demonstrated by years of strenuous effort to gain success. He/she might value romantic love, or family, or wealth, or physical fitness, or the arts, or any and all of the above; if so, his actions in pursuit of these goals, much more than any words, provide corroborating evidence.

Values are always the object of action. They are not mere dreams, wishes, or fantasies.

It is by means of value achievement that a human being, in every form, furthers his/her life. A productive career in a cherished field, for example, both earns an individual the physical necessities of life and adds purpose to his/her existence. The maintenance of close friendships brings intimacy into a person's life; the gaining and sustaining of romantic love adds a form of intimacy both unique and priceless; the rearing of children brings fulfillment to countless millions of parents. Though it be education, career, friendship, bodily or mental health—or one of myriad others—the attainment of rational, healthy, positive, life-sustaining values is the essence of living and living well.

The attainment of values, in other words, does more than enable physical survival and prosperity. Additionally, as a psychological function, the pursuit (and achievement) of values delivers meaning and passion into an individual's life.

Values are the meaning of life.

If Amelia Earhart, for example, was to achieve what the French aptly term "joie de vivre," the joy of living, then she must fly.

Related: In the macrocosm, as well as in the microcosm, human life depends on the achievement of values.

Herbivores prosper by eating grass or berries found on a bush; lions survive by devouring herbivores. But for human beings to survive—and not merely at subsistence level for a truncated lifespan—but to flourish, and to do so for seven decades, or eight, or more—they must cultivate, construct, achieve—they must learn to grow food, to build homes and cities, to cure diseases, to peaceably negotiate intractable disputes, to cultivate the arts, to develop logic and rational philosophy, to create and advance the sciences, and to accomplish vastly more.

Values are the means of life.

Often, their fruition involves dauntlessness and significant prowess on the part of those who trail-blaze them. If, for example, human beings are to achieve safe, convenient, speedy, and global jet travel, then such heroines as Amelia Earhart are necessary to pioneer the activity of flight.

Values Promote Human Life

Further: Values, properly understood, do not subsume goals irrational and life-harming; for example, toxic substances are not a value for a drug addict—loot for a criminal—or authoritarian control for a power luster—although such misguided souls might erroneously deem them so.

Values are beneficial, not inimical to human life.

Because human beings have a definite biological and psychological nature, certain courses of action sustain, while others undermine or terminate their lives. Many foods, for example, provide nutrition, but cyanide yields only death; education promotes knowledge necessary for the prospering of a rational being, but ignorance merely undermines it; liberty unleashes great minds to achieve in every field, but statism imposes repression.

Values, in short, are objective—and are based in the factual requirements of human life.

Ayn Rand identified: "...the fact that living entities exist and function necessitates the existence of values and of an ultimate value which for any living entity is its own life. Thus the validation of value judgments is to be achieved by reference to the facts of reality. The fact that a living entity *is*, determines what it *ought* to do."[32]

That a human being possesses a definite identity means his/her survival and prosperity depend on attainment of specific goals reached by methods distinctive to his nature—and not on or by those appropriate to non-rational beings. "Man's survival *qua* man means the terms, methods, conditions and goals required for the survival of a rational being through the whole of his lifespan—in all those aspects of existence which are open to his choice."[33]

Many things are open to human choice; optional alternatives abound; but we are free neither to choose our nature nor the factual requirements of our lives. "Man cannot survive as anything but man. He *can* abandon his means of survival, his mind, he *can* turn himself into a subhuman creature and he *can* turn his life into a brief span of agony.... But he *cannot* succeed, as a subhuman, in achieving anything but the subhuman—as the ugly horror of the antirational periods of mankind's history can demonstrate."[34]

This is not to say that all human beings do or should hold identical values in every respect. Nature requires human beings to be productive, for example—but whether as butcher, baker, candlestick maker— or as plumber, physician, nuclear physicist—is an optional matter.

Similarly, romantic love is a psychological (and biological) need, whose fulfillment enriches and whose absence depletes an individual's fulfillment—but with Melissa, Maria, or Madeline (or Robert, Raymond, or Ronald, as the case may be) is a matter of personal preference. In a broad philosophic sense, given human nature, values advance man's life—but within such expansive parameters exist discretionary alternatives rich and varied.

A value, to an individual, is something that: 1. objectively promotes human life and 2. is personally cherished by that individual.

Because values are both the means and the meaning of life, they are to be pursued, gained, achieved, realized; never to be surrendered, sacrificed, betrayed, or relinquished.

Heroes as Value Achievers

Heroes are always value-pursuers, value-gainers, value-achievers, and value-realizers; never value-surrenderers, value-sacrificers, value-betrayers, or value-relinquishers. There are no exceptions.

The careers of our three primary real-life examples illustrate this theme.

Maria Montessori held a brilliant vision of the goals she sought to implement. To elevate the methods and materials available to develop a child's independent critical faculty, to more effectively cultivate the young mind, to enhance thinking skills, to advance the intellectual self-sufficiency of mankind's youth—these were the values to which she devoted her career. Not intellectual challenges nor social prejudices nor dictatorial regimes were allowed to thwart her purposes.

Similarly, George Washington Carver devoted his career to science, to discovery of new knowledge, to pushing back cognitive frontiers. Neither intellectual difficulty nor racial bigotry were permitted to halt progress toward culmination of such lofty goals.

Ernest Shackleton, Secretary of the Scottish Royal Geographic Society, undertook several quests to explore previously uncharted quadrants of the earth, to make scientific discoveries, to increase humanity's awareness of its home planet. In his primary purpose of pushing back frontiers of knowledge regarding the world (and, ultimately, the physical universe that humans inhabit) Shackleton stood in a noble line of descent stretching from long before Henry the Navigator to the manned space missions of the 20th and 21st centuries—and beyond. Obstacles, risks, and life-threatening dangers, to explorers, are insufficient reasons to abandon expeditions of discovery. "Difficulties are just things to overcome, afterall,"[35] stated Shackleton.

Education, science, exploration—these were personal loves to such heroes. These values animated their lives. No matter the effort or degree of difficulty required, these values were to be achieved, not surrendered.

An inviolable commitment to values that sustain and/or further human life is the foundation of heroism.

Nevertheless, there is a widespread belief that heroism involves not self-fulfillment, but its antipode—self-sacrifice; indeed, the conviction that self-sacrifice constitutes the essence of heroism.

Such a belief is false, even pernicious, and an issue so important that several chapters are required to provide it a proper treatment.

CHAPTER SEVEN

Virtue and Self-Sacrifice as Moral Antagonists

The conventional understanding of heroism often—perhaps generally—construes selflessness or self-sacrifice as a cardinal element. A paradigm example is a soldier, in combat, throwing himself—to save his comrades—on a live grenade, knowing that death is the certain result. In specific contexts, this is indubitably a heroic act; but to the extent that it—or any action—is heroic, to that extent it exempts itself from the status of self-sacrificial.

The essential point can be succinctly stated: Heroism involves the creation and/or defense of values; self-sacrifice the surrender of them.

Heroes are a sub-category of morally upright persons. Morally upright persons do not sacrifice themselves.

A Heroic Story

Let us begin discussion of this issue by examining the actions of a hero already mentioned: George Washington.

During the American War of Independence, Washington faced monumental challenges to keep alive American military resistance.

He had to organize and train an army, he often faced seasoned British commanders and troops, his forces at times were heavily outnumbered, he lost numerous battles, his small army dwindled further through desertion, and members of Congress sought to replace him as commander of the Continental Army.

Further, at Valley Forge, Washington and his army suffered through a withering winter in 1778 in which disease, exposure, and malnutrition killed roughly 2500 American soldiers out of an army totaling merely 11,000–12,000.

Washington expressed forthrightly the misery of the predicament: "For some days past there has been a famine in camp ... A part of the army has been a week without any kind of flesh ... Naked and starving as they are, we cannot enough admire the ... fidelity of the soldiery, that they have not been ... excited by their sufferings to a general mutiny..."[36]

When patriotic Americans refer to the "sacrifices" made by America's Founders, these are the types of examples to which they refer.

The terrible privations suffered, the less wretched and dangerous life forgone, the peace, security, and comfort forsaken, so many values relinquished—even, in many cases, life itself—none of these can be doubted. All of these goods surrendered in quest of liberty: In this context, in pursuit of such a goal, do such values forsworn constitute a sacrifice?

The Meaning of Sacrifice

An excellent way to begin answering the question is to arrive at a definition of the term "sacrifice." What, precisely, does it mean to *sacrifice* the self? The pertinent definition offered by the *American Heritage Dictionary*, 5th edition, states: "The act of giving up something highly valued for the sake of something else considered to have a greater value or claim. *Social activism often involves tremendous sacrifice."*

This is a puzzling definition: For if an individual, in giving up something highly valued, receives in exchange something of even greater value, the exchange is then self-interested, not self-sacrificing. For example, a person who prizes a superb education more highly than a great sum of money—and then allocates that sum to attain such an education. In terms of his own values, this is a net gain, perhaps a substantial one, not a loss. In what sense, then, can this transaction properly be considered a "sacrifice?"

Perhaps a lesser dictionary will provide a better definition. *Webster's Collegiate Dictionary*, 11th edition, defines sacrifice as: "destruction or surrender of something for the sake of something else."

"For the sake of something else"—what does this mean? If a college student, for example, surrenders drinking for the sake of his/her studies, is that a sacrifice? Is it to be assumed that knowledge has less value to human life—or to this particular human being—than carousing?

If there were an all-knowing, all-powerful being who mandated that college students choose—surrender one, retain one—and the overwhelming preponderance opted to continue their studies—as they would—do they personally value drinking more, but sacrifice it in dutiful service to their parents? Or do they themselves assess education as of greater long-term worth than carousing? If the latter, as this writer suspects, is that a sacrifice?

Does this mean that if a person gives up a penny for a dollar, illness for health, or ignorance for wisdom—he/she has made a sacrifice? On the *Webster* definition, this would be a reasonable construal. The problem wreaking havoc with such a definition is its utter lack of value assessment—no mention of the relative worth—to the individual performing the "surrender"—of either the thing surrendered or the one gained. Consequently, the definition is too vague to be of service.

Another offering from the same source states: "to suffer loss of, give up, renounce, injure, or destroy esp. for an ideal, belief, or end." But the same problem persists: What if the "ideal, belief, or end" means more to the "sacrificing" individual than does the thing "suffer[ed] loss of, give[n] up, renounced, injured, or destroyed?"

If a freedom fighter, for example—who above all prizes liberty from a tyrannical oppressor—loses, in the ensuing struggle, every scintilla of material wealth but gains freedom, is this properly construed as a "sacrifice"? Conventionally, it might well be so regarded. But this again involves insufficient attention paid to the relative value—to the acting agent—of the things lost and gained.

Ayn Rand provided a precise answer to the dilemma: "A 'sacrifice' is the surrender of a value ... for the sake of a lesser value or of a nonvalue..."[37] Presumably, on Rand's view, self-interest entails, in the face of such alternative, pursuit of the higher value—a persistent refusal to surrender or repudiate it.

George Washington Carver, for example, might have surrendered the rigors of scientific discovery for the less demanding career of teaching students information already known. He might also have left Tuskegee and the Jim Crow South for life in the racially-less-bigoted North. But he did not.

Presumably, such surrender would have enhanced the ease of life but not its meaning; the creative agricultural work, best done at Tuskegee, was of supreme significance; everything else of lesser importance. So Carver's refusal to surrender that of greater value to him for something of lesser value was action self-fulfilling, not self-sacrificing. In brief, he remained loyal to his ruling purpose, declining to betray it.

Conversely, if, in any form, Carver had surrendered the creative work that was the principal source of meaning in his life, if he had done such for any reason, this would have constituted a sacrifice and a major one.

Loyalty in action, regardless obstacles or challenges, to one's most cherished values—this is the essence of moral rectitude—and it is the foundation of heroism.

The Value of Personal Relationships

This is as true of intimate relationships as it is of career goals. Close personal relations, like achievements in education and career, are substantial values.

The immense importance to an individual of intimate relationships is often misunderstood. Therefore, the place occupied by another human being at or near the pinnacle of an individual's personal value hierarchy is misunderstood. Consequently, taking actions supportive of a cherished other is often conventionally–and mistakenly—construed as self-sacrificing.

In every day terms, consider the confusion surrounding the relationship between conscientious, loving parents and their children. The "sacrifices" made by such parents are often pointed out.

Let us say that the parents wanted to buy a beautiful home in the suburbs but could not afford to because of the expense of sending their children to an excellent private school. They might have instead sent the kids to public schools, thereby saving a good deal of money, which could have formed part of a down payment on the desired home. Because they therefore proceed to make do with a lesser home, it is said of them that they made "sacrifices" for the children.

But a resounding objection to this understanding, simply phrased, is that the parents love their children vastly more than they do a fine home—that they value the children's well-being substantially beyond the comforts of gracious living—and that their happiness is enhanced a thousand-fold by the fulfillment of one over the other.

Assuming clean, safe, comfortable quarters already enjoyed by the children, the question raised by such conscientious parents is: An upgrade in education or an improvement in living arrangements—which, now and in the long run, will more significantly enhance the child's life? The child is a monumental value in the parent's life—his or her well-being is of supreme importance.

The choice to spend the money on the children's education, rather than on a more spacious home, is made in accordance with their values; the choice is utterly value-laden and value-driven.

Given the value significance of the children in their lives, and granted their assessment of education as more conducive than a new home to the children's well-being, a choice to deploy the money on behalf of education is self-fulfilling; it is made in pursuit of a higher rather than a lower value. Conversely, a choice to purchase the home would be self-sacrificing; it would entail surrendering a higher value for a lesser one.

To do good for someone valued, cherished, deeply loved is to do good for oneself.

Surely, over the millennia, many human beings have identified this truth regarding relationships with their children, their lover or spouse, their dearest friends, and/or others.

Let us raise the following question to those who are, in our judgment, the most diligent parents: What would make you happier—the health and fulfillment of your child, though conjoined with few material possessions on your part—or sickness and pain for the child combined with your acquisition of significant material wealth?

The great preponderance of parents—especially those most responsible—will properly invoke the alternative benefiting their child. Such loving parents gain greater happiness from their child's well-being than from material wealth because the child is of vastly greater importance to them. Therefore, actions benefitting the child, although hurting the parents' bank balances, are self-interested, not self-sacrificing ones.

To illustrate: Would a family of modest means sell their beloved child for five million dollars? If so, would the material wealth make them happier than the child's loving presence? Most such families would refuse the deal; the rest would regret it. To relinquish the child for material wealth would be to surrender a higher value for—in this case, not a non-value—but a lesser value. Pain and suffering, not joy and fulfillment, will be the inevitable result. (If money were more important to these parents, would the overwhelming majority of them pay ransom, sometimes large amounts, for the safe return of a kidnapped child?)

The same principle, in a different form, is true of other important persons in an individual's life. When a man gives up a cherished apartment and a good deal of money to place a down payment on a house—that he may or may not desire—but that his fiancée does—it is because he values her happiness more highly than possession of the apartment or the cash. His soon-to-be-wife—and the love they share—is, understandably, to him, much more important than the other values.

Similarly, if an individual gives up a relaxing weekend of golf, flies across country, and rents a hotel room, so that he may attend a dear friend's wedding—the activities forsworn, the time taken, and the money spent are secondary; his friend's well-being, and the joy taken in that well-being, are paramount. The effort he expends to share such a momentous event is an indicator, in action, of the friend's cherished place in his life.

Such examples can be endlessly replicated regarding an individual's dearest friends, lover, and family members.

For a rational individual, seeking prospering human life, other human beings represent enormous boon—as family, educators, friends, colleagues, lover, spouse, children—at least as much of a benefit as career advance, financial gain, and upgraded material conditions.

Closeness with such persons is an authentic value not to be minimally esteemed—and favoring them is a form of benefiting oneself. To maintain that aiding them is a form of self-sacrifice is an egregious and insulting denigration of their stature in one's life. Abetting those one loves is a form of being true to oneself.

The conventional understanding is that it is sacrificial to surrender, for esteemed others, such things as apartments, money, golf trips, and so forth. Consider the enormity of the insult.

Here is the essence of the conventional view expressed regarding a person's attitude toward—let us say—his child: "I would rather take the money spent on your education and, with it, buy a boat. I would prefer to take the time spent with you at the park and, with it, watch baseball. I do not love you very much—I do these things for and with you, because, as your parent, it is my duty. Your well-being and happiness are minimal values to me—but I sacrifice—for you—the things and persons that, to me, are of greater significance."

A child would properly recoil in horror from such parental attitude. He/she would feel unloved, under-valued, and unhappy. He would have every right to loathe such parents.

By contrast, a rational understanding—and that lived out, in reality, by millions and millions of parents (and persons in other close relationships)—is described above. It may be expressed: "You (child, spouse, dear friend) are of supreme importance to me—in my life you are at or near the acme of my personal value pantheon—there is virtually nothing that, done for you, would be a sacrifice; or, alternatively phrased, there is very little that I would not gladly do for you. Doing for you is the same as doing for me—for, to me, you are that important."

This is Shane's attitude toward the Starrett family, all of them— Joe, Marian, and Bobby. He dearly, desperately wants to give up gun-fighting, violence, bloodshed, and the horror of these. But if he does, Joe Starrett will be murdered, Marian widowed, Bobby semi-orphaned. Bobby will lose the proper role model he requires to become a peaceful man of non-violent productivity.

Observe the bitterly ironic, inner value conflict for Shane: To save the man of peace requires the former man of violence to revert. For Bobby to grow up hero worshiping the man of peace requires the gunfighter to perform a protective act of violence worthy of hero worship. Even if Shane succeeds in saving Joe's life, he risks supplanting Joe in Bobby's vision of heroism.

Nevertheless, all of this pales. He cannot let Joe be killed.

Without a doubt, Shane gives up a great deal. *A great deal.* But it is not of as much value to him as the safety of the persons he loves most in the world. Properly, both joyfully and painfully, Shane chooses that (or those) whom he values most above that which he values substantially but less.

A sacrifice is surrendering a higher value for a lesser value or a nonvalue. This, Shane refuses to do.

Close relationships with other human beings are emphatically among life's most significant values.

As such, they are to be pursued, gained, cherished; never voluntarily abandoned.

A huge part, for example, of Odysseus's heroism is his relentless homeward drive, his unyielding determination to win back to his beloved wife, Penelope, and the son he has never met. To attain such a goal, he battles storms, fights monsters, struggles against the wrath of a god, and more. Although such grueling quest was fictional, the tale Homer so vividly depicts packs the emotional wallop it does because of the place held by romantic love and family in the value pantheon of numberless human beings. For any number of readers, Odysseus's value quest resonates and rings true.

More important, given the intimacy and joy that romantic love and family can bring into an honest person's life, it is right and proper that Odysseus and many others value it so highly.

The achievement of values in all fields, including intimate relations with trusted others, is the essence of self-fulfillment.

The abandonment, surrender, or betrayal of values is the essence of self-sacrifice.

Heroes—like Odysseus—always seek value achievement.

A Narrow, Mistaken Understanding of Self-Interest

Related, a long-standing moral belief—and a profound error—is of a supposed dichotomy between doing for self and doing for others. Helping oneself regarding values that do not (at a superficial glance) directly help others, for example, career advance, financial gain, and the like, is recognized as self-interested. But helping others, including persons dear, whose happiness is of central importance, is not so recognized.

Too often, human beings—both those who applaud self-interest and those who deplore it—mistakenly construe it in a severely delimited form: As though it consists primarily, even exclusively of financial gain.

The truth is that wealth earned by means of one's own mind and effort is a substantial boon that significantly facilitates one's life; without doubt, it is a proper value—but it is by no means the only one.

Education is likewise a profound benefit, in quest of which persons often—and properly—expend large sums of material wealth. Mental health is an immense boon—as are fitness and bodily health. Friendship is a significant value—love even more so—and children, for billions, a priceless one. The attainment of material wealth is one—although by no means the sole—form of seeking one's self-interest.

To reiterate: The pursuit of goals that are, simultaneously, objectively life-enhancing and personally cherished—this is the essence of self-interested action.

There is no inherent moral dichotomy in human life between doing for self and doing for others. It is not the case that whereas pursuing career advance is self-interested, helping loved ones is not—and perhaps is even self-sacrificing. This belief can be exposed as erroneous in several forms.

The Harmony of Self-Fulfillment and Helping Others

It is a simple matter to help both self and others, and honest human beings accomplish this many times daily.

Take as one example, an individual's pursuit of career success. He/she is, let us say, a high school English teacher; he loves literature, and passionately communicates such love to his students; he reads, studies, and enhances his teaching skills; he devotes spare time to tutoring students who seek it; and so forth. Such an active career benefits him—he earns an honest living, takes in it significant pride, and, above all, fills his work hours with what he most loves.

At the same time, via the identical actions, he/she significantly benefits others: In facilitating understanding of great stories, appreciation of superb writing, insights into human motivation, nature, and life, and upgrades in writing skills, he substantially aids his students (that, over the course of a career, might number thousands). Further, by contributing to their well-being, he benefits all those who love the students—for example, their parents. This example can be replicated countless times by reference to numerous productive careers.

Related: Examine an honest person's cultivation of character. He/she realizes that, although it is good to be intelligent—to be athletic—to be good-looking—and so forth—the highest good in human life, the most significant form of strength, is: strength of character.

Such an individual diligently takes responsibility for his/her choices and actions, even when so doing is painful in the short-term. He is unfailingly truthful, although, on occasion, for some, the truth might be hurtful. He is utterly trustworthy—those in his purview confidently entrust him with their lives and even those of their children.

The practical outcome? His/her unfailing commitment to personal responsibility, in the long term, engenders significant educational and career success. His trustworthiness enhances intimate relations with like-minded souls. His unbreached honesty creates conscience unperturbed and spirit unruffled. He benefits substantially. Do others?

His/her employers, customers, or clients gain from his conscientious work ethic. His friends, spouse, children, family, and acquaintances, from his trustworthiness. Those seeking fair dealing and/or honest judgment, from his truthfulness—and so on.

Human beings benefit innocent others to the extent they manifest strong character; wrong the good, to the extent they suffer from its lack. It is not through honesty, integrity, or personal responsibility that persons wrong their peers—but via the negation of such.

The character strengths that promote prospering self are the identical ones that promote such a self's positive impact in the lives of others.

For a heroic instance of this, we can return to the career of George Washington, whose unbending integrity was widely recognized and admired, including by political foes; resulting in an unopposed selection as the nation's first President, and in felicitous consequences for the fledgling republic. Washington's widely recognized character strength abetted both himself and innumerable other honest Americans.

Self-Fulfillment, Not Self-Sacrifice, is a Practical Benefit to Others

As a practical point: It is an individual's genuine self-fulfillment that benefits others, not his or her self-sacrifice. This is especially true of the heroes with whom this book is concerned.

Shakespeare is a representative example of the principle. Presumably, his self-fulfillment lay in exercising his literary capacities, in nurturing them, in composing magnificent drama and poetry, in acting, in full immersion in the related worlds of theater and literature. Via his own flourishing, he created a body of work that, for four centuries, has immeasurably enriched the lives of numberless millions.

Let us perform a thought experiment: What if he had relinquished such a life—whether voluntarily caring for dying relatives, or coercively serving in the crown's armed forces, or one of another myriad forms of self-sacrifice? If a person surrenders his vision—if he yields that of greater importance for that of lesser—if he persistently cedes the self—then not happiness but misery is the inescapable result.

Shakespeare's existence is thereby reduced from self-development and joy to self-surrender and pain—and the existence of his brothers and sisters, across the ages, is deprived of majestic art works that could illuminate it.

Authentic self-sacrifice is a lose-lose proposition.

Even those for whom sacrifices are specifically made do not benefit from them.

Let us imagine that Shakespeare did surrender his career to tend to sick relatives. Do they love him? Do they not see his suffering—or do they not care? *Genuine good will for another lies in supporting his/ her pursuit of values*—never in requesting, much less demanding those values be sacrificed. If they are persons of good will, they are necessarily pained by their relative's misery ... a pain re-doubled by realization that they are a prime cause of it.

A much more benevolent—and effective—solution is to exhort Shakespeare: Care for us insofar as you love us—but do what you must to enhance your career—write by candlelight in the evening—slip down to London on weekends, when relief is forthcoming—maintain relations with your theater colleagues—network—plot out your triumphant return—but, whatever you do, do not betray your gifts—because we love you, and we want only success and fulfillment for you. In brief, care for us, not as a sacrifice, but because you love us, and want good things for us—as we love and desire the best for you.

Properly helping others is—and should be—a win-win, non-sacrificial action.

Thomas Edison, as a second example, toiled inexorably in the field he dearly loved—inventing—creating finally a commercially viable incandescent electric light (and a plethora of other devices.) Such achievement earned him not merely substantial financial profit but also, more meaningfully, fulfillment from a cherished career over the course of a lifetime. His value creation led to incalculable benefit for untold millions of human beings.

What would have been the result of sacrificing such values? The result would be dual: 1. Edison's personal misery. 2. Mankind's deprivation of supremely important values.

(That if Edison had not reached the achievements he did, someone else would have, is a claim most likely true. But such arduous accomplishments would have been gained by someone equally devoted to the craft, an individual of identical passion who steadfastly refused to betray or sacrifice his life's work—this claim is also true.)

The underlying reason can now be made clear: Values support human life. Therefore, an individual's creation of them benefits many, himself or herself first, foremost, and always; his surrender or betrayal of them hurts many, pre-eminently himself or herself.

The value of values is that they sustain life—for any and all who fall within the compass of their creation. It is their creation that benefits human life, not their surrender.

One key point is stronger and deeper than: There is no necessary dichotomy between fulfilling the self and helping others.

The point is: There is a necessary dichotomy between sacrificing the self and helping others.

Good Will and Self-Sacrifice Are Moral Antitheses

It is among the worst tragedies of human life—historically and currently—that human beings so often equate self-sacrifice with goodwill. Such an equation is false, and worse—it is pernicious.

Self-sacrifice and benevolence are not equivalent or even congruent attributes. Rather, they are mutually exclusive qualities.

The incisive question that exposes the antithesis is: *Where is the kindness for those called upon to sacrifice themselves?* Where, for example, is the goodwill for the man drafted, against his will, into the military, on the moral ground that he must sacrifice—perhaps life itself—for the nation? Where for an aspiring professional woman demanded to surrender her cherished career to satisfy the norms upheld in her suppressive culture? Where for the young person exhorted to sacrifice his/her romantic love to meet the expectations of the family?

Why—to apply Shakespeare's immortal phrase—is "the milk of human kindness" not extended to such innocent, in many cases, morally exemplary persons?

Perhaps another question must be antecedently answered: If virtue resides in sacrifice for others, how could such kindness be so extended?

For human beings to be good, on such a code, they must diligently perform their unchosen duty. If they shirk, they are morally delinquent. Therefore, on a self-sacrifice creed, human beings must obediently shoulder their ordained moral burdens. In important respects, others—not themselves—dictate the terms and the course of their lives.

The self-sacrifice ethic, consistently deployed, requires good persons to surrender their priceless loves. Afterall, if what one surrenders has little or no value to the surrenderer, it is not a sacrifice. If a practicing Catholic, who dislikes vegetables, relinquishes spinach for Lent, it is not a sacrifice. An authentic sacrifice is of an authentic value.

Consistently imposed, such an ethic exhorts human beings to sacrifice their education, their career, their romantic love, their children, their dearest friends, and so forth.

By contrast, goodwill toward another human being involves: 1. awareness of that person's value hierarchy 2. support of the person's values. If someone, for example, loves books on science and is bored by puzzles, then science books and not puzzles make an appropriate present for that individual. A more momentous example is: If a college student genuinely loves literature and desires a career as an English teacher, then the parents, after being rebuffed when sincerely encouraging medicine, should support the child's choice and not demand the child sacrifice it in favor of their preference. As a further illustration, the popular 2002 film, *Bend It Like Beckham*, depicted an immigrant family initially rejecting but then supporting their athletic daughter's choice to play college soccer rather than following a life in accordance with their old country traditions. This affecting story showed the parents coming to properly accept and then uphold their daughter's cherished values.

Goodwill or benevolence toward others lies in support of their life-affirming values—not in opposition to these—not in calling upon others to sacrifice their values.

Conversely, in many cases, the self-sacrifice code, if consistently employed, involves demanding that innocent persons surrender their cherished values.

Do the advocates of so monstrous a code care regarding the unrelieved misery they thereby inflict on mankind's most conscientious members—on those who seek to do right as they have been taught to construe it?

The Self-Sacrifice Code Writ Large

Look at the results of this code in the macrocosm, at the social, not just at the personal level: No atrocity is so egregious that it cannot be supported by the call for self-sacrifice. Who, for example, are the worst mass murderers of history? The Communists and National Socialists (Nazis) who, between them, by conservative estimate, slaughtered 120 million innocent civilians.[38]

What moral code—to them—justified mass murder? That, in differing forms, a person's life belongs not to him/her but to the state, that it may be disposed of as the state deems fit, and that individuals must make sacrifices, including the supreme one, if it is judged beneficial to the state's welfare. The "wisdom" of the Cambodian Communists (who butchered twenty-five percent of the nation's population in three-and-a-half years) expressed to each individual was: "Losing you is not a loss, and keeping you is no specific gain."[39]

An individual, in other words, in and of himself/herself, possesses no value. He/she gains such only via willingness to sacrifice for the state—that is, to others on a grand scale.

Hitler makes related points.

Why did National Socialists regard the Aryans as a superior race? Hitler explains that their reasons are on moral grounds:

"This self-sacrificing will to give one's personal labor and if necessary one's own life for others is most strongly developed in the Aryan.

The Aryan is not greatest in his mental qualities as such, but in the extent of his willingness to put all his abilities in service of the community. In him the instinct of self-preservation has reached the noblest form, since he willingly subordinates his own ego to the life of the community and, if the hour demands, even sacrifices it."[40]

The basic moral code from which such selfless action proceeds, Hitler states, "we call—to distinguish it from egoism and selfishness—idealism. By this we understand only the individual's capacity to make sacrifices for the community, for his fellow men."[41]

In this, National Socialism willingly followed the political teachings of leading German philosopher, G.W.F. Hegel: "A single person is something subordinate, and as such he must dedicate himself to the ethical whole. Hence if the state claims life, the individual must surrender it."[42]

Why did the National Socialists demonize the Jews? "In the Jewish people the will to self-sacrifice does not go beyond the individual's naked instinct of self-preservation.... His [the Jew's] sense of sacrifice is only apparent.... Here again the Jew is led by nothing but the naked egoism of the individual."[43]

Here is seen the full, logical conclusion of the creed opposing self-interest: The self, the individual human being, manifests moral worth only insofar as, in some form, he/she serves others (in macrocosm, the state); in and of himself/herself, in his own being, he possesses none.

Indeed, an anti-self-interest moral code is logically grounded in a philosophy that esteems only something "higher"—whether God or the state—than an individual, who exists solely to serve the more exalted being.

Pursuing *self*-interest can be considered wrong only if, and because, the self is considered base. Why should an individual's self be considered base while the collective—a group of individual selves—is considered of value? There is no logical answer to this question. In truth, every individual human life, in and of itself, is of immense value.

The Contradiction of the Self-Sacrifice Code

Among other problems, there is a logical contradiction in this moral theory. If virtue lies only in selfless service—and if self-fulfilling action is dishonorable—then what is the moral status of a recipient of charitable action? On what motive—other than self-interest—does he/she accept another's largesse?

But if self-interested action is considered "selfish" and ignoble, how is it right for the charity-provider to engage in such action? How can his/her virtue depend on another's vice? How can it be morally upright for him/her to aid and abet selfishness? Or is self-interest on the part of the recipient actually good? Rand states the point with searing clarity:

"Why is it moral to serve the happiness of others, but not your own? If enjoyment is a value, why is it moral when experienced by others, but immoral when experienced by you? If the sensation of eating a cake is a value, why is it an immoral indulgence in your stomach, but a moral goal for you to achieve in the stomach of others? Why is it immoral for you to desire, but moral for others to do so? Why is it immoral to produce a value and keep it, but moral to give it away? And if it is not moral for you to keep a value, why is it moral for others to accept it? If you are selfless and virtuous when you give it, are they not selfish and vicious when they take it? Does virtue consist of serving vice? Is the moral purpose of those who are good, self-immolation for the sake of those who are evil?"[44]

Related, the recipient—call him Bill James—on this code, can properly receive from another aid that he cannot properly provide himself. Why? Why is it noble when Tom Smith provides Bill James food—but "selfish" and wrong when James earns it for himself? As contrasted to receiving charity from others, does his life devolve into diminished value when and because he earns the self-same goods for himself?

The self-sacrifice creed generates a weird ethos regarding the value of an individual human life: It is of great worth, such that others can and should properly help him—but of so little worth that he/she cannot properly help himself/herself. An individual life is of value—but is not of value. Herein lies another version of the logical contradiction intrinsic to a self-sacrifice code.

Why is it considered wrong for an individual to better himself/herself? In fact, whatever the depredations of humanity's moral beliefs, helping innocent others—a person's brothers and sisters—is good, because human life is sacred. For the exact reason, it is proper for a person to help himself/herself.

After-all, if Bill James awakes thirsty in the dead of night, should he cross the yard, rouse his neighbor, and request a glass of water—or should he get it himself? A person is generally best suited to help himself—and the same preciousness of life that justifies another's generosity to him ennobles his own aid to himself.

Finally, looked at from a different perspective: To another, you are the other. If your life is sufficiently important for him/her to nurture, surely it is of requisite value for you to do so. The life of an honest person is a value, regardless whose actions enhance it.

Summary

A number of points discussed in this chapter should now be clear: 1. Helping others dear to a person constitutes a form of rationally self-interested action 2. There is no necessary dichotomy between helping self and helping others 3. In properly fulfilling himself, a person helps others in innumerable forms 4. Others benefit from a rational individual's self-fulfillment—nobody benefits from his/her self-sacrifice. 5. Good will toward our brothers and sisters involves supporting their quest for cherished values and never calling upon them to sacrifice these.

CHAPTER EIGHT

Heroism Versus Self-Sacrifice

After this lengthy discussion, an important point can be made directly related to the book's theme: Heroes are valuers. They are value-supporters-and-achievers—not value-betrayers or value-surrenderers.

Their prowess is always—at all times, and with no exceptions—placed in service of values. Take a leading example of the principle.

Examine some of the groundbreaking achievements of Aristotle.

He was profoundly engrossed in questions of philosophy and science—indeed, in the entirety of nature, including human beings and their creations; wisely for himself, and fortunately for humanity, he pursued such fascination over the course of an immensely productive career.

He formulated the rules of proper reasoning, identified the major errors of reasoning—logical fallacies—and taught that proper reasoning is grounded—not in myth, faith-based beliefs, or personal feelings—but in observable facts. It is no exaggeration to state that he, more than any other single person, taught mankind how to think.[45]

For this alone, he should be held as an immortal.

But in addition, he made substantial contributions to every branch of philosophy, pioneered the science of biology,[46] and developed an ethical system urging not self-sacrifice but self-actualization in accordance with mankind's rational nature.

His glorious attainments are the work of fulfilling, not sacrificing, his values. His self-realization is a paramount example of his own moral code.

Because of this, he is one of mankind's grandest heroes.

Other heroes, many already described, provide similar examples of this principle.

Are There Examples of Self-Sacrificing Heroes?

The leading counter-examples to the above argument are of those individuals ceding their lives to protect ideals and/or persons deeply cherished. A parent who, in the act of saving his/her child, surrenders his own life—or a soldier who is killed protecting his comrades—or a man who perishes in support of freedom, his own and/or those of individuals and the country he treasures. These kinds of examples are congruent, we might remember, with one definition of "hero" provided by the *American Heritage Dictionary*: "A person noted for feats of courage or nobility of purpose, especially one who has risked or sacrificed his life: *soldiers and nurses who were heroes in an unpopular war.*"

Such actions, and many similar ones, can be heroic. The question is: Are they self-sacrificing? The answer is a resounding: No.

Perhaps the best explanation begins with a colloquialism: That such-and-such represents "a fate worse than death." What does this popular expression mean? Is it merely an overwrought emotionalist exclamation—or does it possess moral currency? Is it credible?

Its meaning—whether true or false—should be clear: There are calamities to potentially befall a person that may, rationally and with good reason, be assessed worse than dying.

Is this, in fact, true? Are there such calamities?

Indeed. Life is precious not for the sake of eating, digesting, and sleeping; these are means to an end, the things rational persons do to sustain themselves along the path of their lives. But the path of their lives—properly—is the achievement of values passionately held. What if some implacable force irrevocably and eternally prohibited them from ever pursuing the value(s) that filled with meaning their lives?

Answers To The Counter-Examples

Conduct the following thought experiment: Young Amelia Earhart grows up not in America but under a dictatorship, similar to the Taliban (or ISIS), that utterly suppresses the rights of women. Sensing her defiant spirit, and regarding flight utterly inappropriate to women, the dictators offer her the following diabolic alternative:

"You may continue to live, you may eat, socialize, marry, and so forth, but you will never set foot in a plane, much less pilot one. You are eternally prohibited from flying, even as a passenger, never mind as a pilot. Secret police officers will follow you every moment of your existence, waking and sleeping, they will forcibly prevent you from approaching within miles of an airfield or airplane, they will observe and restrain you every second of your life until your last, expiring breath. Or we will kill you right now or, at your discretion, at some subsequent time. Which is it to be?"

Related, the tyrants might go further. What if they forbade her to marry or have a romantic relationship of any kind? What if the secret police officers assigned to surveil her were fiendishly instructed to prohibit close friendships? That is, if the dictators enforced inalterable extirpation of life's top two or three values, the luckless victim has little left for which to live.

Would anyone be surprised if Amelia Earhart, under those conditions, chose death? Or if, remaining alive, she lapsed into a living death of stuporous lethargy, lacking all vigor or enterprise? Especially if, after a period of time, she realized the power and relentlessness of the oppressor would not abate, and this was her fate for the remaining years and decades of her life. Given certainty of eternally enforced eradication of one's ruling passion(s), is life truly preferable to death?

(Yes, it is, if one can escape. But such assessment rests on the hope that, elsewhere, the meaningful value(s) might be restored. What if such hope is conclusively demonstrated to be groundless?)

Under conditions of such encompassing value repression, rational human beings would be appalled by the dictators' cruelty, not by Amelia Earhart's understandable selection of death.

Life is precious for those who fill it with passionately-held values. Every waking moment is an opportunity to progress toward a cherished goal; eating and sleeping enables the body to remain fresh; entertainment re-fuels the soul; these are but necessary means to an end.

Such a person experiences life as purposeful motion toward a shining conclusion, and this process, the entirety of it—both the goal and the striving—provides fiercely held, uniquely-personal meaning that enables indomitable perseverance and, ultimately, triumph over vicissitude and life's inevitable heartbreaks.

Subtract—irrevocably—from an individual's life the things or persons that provide it meaning, and what remains? Meaninglessness.

It is neither the case that life's purpose derives from participation in a divinely-ordained plan, nor that, in the absence of such design, existence is necessarily experienced as listlessly-unbearable ennui. Self-chosen values are the meaning-maker in a person's life.

Heroes, at least at an implicit level, understand this. They stop at nothing to create and/or protect values. This is the actual meaning of the examples cited above. A parent throwing himself/herself in front of a bus, dying heroically in the act of saving his/her child, has not sacrificed a value: *He has protected one.*

If such a parent had time to make a value calculation prior to action, it would reason like this: If someone must die, what outcome—for me—will be the least inimical—the continuation of my life in the irrevocable absence of my child—or the continuation of my child's life in the absence of mine?

The child's well-being is so momentous a value to such a parent—so monumental an aspect of life's purpose—that his/her inalterable loss is necessarily experienced as meaning-crushing. The world is thereby emptied, the sun eclipsed, the passion drained, the meaning annulled. Life is unremitting pain.

This is not to say that such a parent will then necessarily end his/her life; it is to say that, given a brutal choice, his/her values lead him to save the child.

The discussion may end with the military examples raised in the previous chapter.

Military Counter-Examples

To George Washington and the other American heroes of Valley Forge, such death-dealing conditions were faced in indomitable commitment to liberty. The inalienable right to life, liberty, and the pursuit of happiness spoken of so eloquently by Thomas Jefferson stood as a beacon in the minds of such men. They understood the shining ideal—the spirit of '76—for which they fought. Other considerations, even risk of life—even its loss—were subordinate. Every one, they realized, must die. But does every one die in unshakeable commitment to a personally-sacred cause? Their actions were laden with and driven by values.

To such men, who held dear their own liberty and that of the persons and nascent republic they loved, the surrender of liberty—not the surrender of life on its behalf—would constitute a sacrifice.

Samuel Sharpe, heroic black leader of a Jamaican slave rebellion in 1831, facing execution, uttered the immortal words: "I would rather die on yonder gallows than live in slavery."[47]

Sharpe understood the explanatory principle: Death is an alternative superior to interminable life in chains. Under such conditions, death is not a sacrifice: Rather, it is a release.

Finally, what of a soldier who throws himself upon a live grenade to save his comrades? Such an act is heroic in certain contexts—but is not to be inherently and automatically assessed as such without qualification.

Heroism is always action in service of values and life—not in service of destruction and death. For example, regardless the prowess and death-defying exploits of an SS officer committed to the principles of National Socialism, there is no heroism—no moral probity—in fighting for mass murder.

But an individual may fight for morally superior reasons—to defend freedom, to protect family and loved ones, to rid a beloved homeland of foreign invaders, and so forth. He is on a mission; the task at hand serves his goal; his comrades are indispensable facilitators; their lives are vital to the mission's success, and must be protected.

He rises up, he stands tall to save them and to keep alive hope of ultimate victory. In effect, he fights to the death in service of liberty. His life is given to further his values, in honor of all that—to him—is sacred; it is what makes the action noble.

Conversely, does it become honorably magnanimous by virtue of surrendering or betraying his values—by sacrificing that which, in his life, is reverential? If liberty is dear, for example, but he relinquishes it for thirty pieces of silver (or some such secondary value), would such a sacrificial action be heroic?

No. Surrendering that which makes life meaningful makes life meaningless, not fulfilled; such self-sacrifice serves suffering, not joy; it furthers misery and death, not happiness and life. It is a betrayal of life and the steps, sometimes onerous, necessary to advance it. As such, it is cowardly, not heroic.

Related, is it heroic to surrender life for the sake of that which, to the surrenderer, is inconsequential?

If it were the case that, for the soldier, liberty was of minor importance, and/or his comrades but casual acquaintances, and/or their causal role in facilitating triumph was negligible—so that he surrendered life for trivialities or non-values—this would indubitably be self-sacrifice.

Would such an action be heroic?

No, sacrificing life for inconsequential details is to spit in the face of life's importance.

A hero risks life only for values momentously significant to him/ her.

It is not necessarily a sacrifice to surrender one's life. It is always a sacrifice to surrender the values that make one's life meaningful.

"If you wish to save the last of your dignity, do not call your best actions a 'sacrifice': that term brands you as immoral."[48]

In truth, a person's "best actions" are value-laden and value-driven. An individual achieves the exalted status of heroism by refusal, under any and all circumstances, to surrender his/her most prized values; standing for them even, when necessary, to the death.

CHAPTER NINE

Anti-Heroes

The phenomenon of anti-heroism pervades modern culture.

The Nature of Anti-Heroism

Anti-heroism is an intellectual, largely literary phenomenon that is often confused with villainy. Such conflation is an error, and the key differences readily explained: 1. Villains are evil—anti-heroes are merely ineffectual 2. Villains oppose heroes—anti-heroes simply lack heroism. The appellation of "anti-heroism" is a misnomer; the phenomenon it identifies should properly be labeled: "non-heroism"—or, dropping the negation, "human fecklessness."

One on-line source defines "antihero" as: "a leading character in a film, book or play who lacks the traditional heroic qualities such as idealism, courage, nobility, fortitude, [and] moral goodness..."[49] The source continues: "Whereas the classical hero is larger than life, antiheroes are typically inferior to the reader in intelligence, dynamism, or ... purpose..."[50]

This is an excellent formulation that requires no revision. Serious twentieth-century literature—whether novels, dramas, films—are dominated by such a phenomenon. The character of Willy Loman in Arthur

Miller's play, *Death of a Salesman*, is a representative example. He is an exhausted and ultimately failed traveling salesman, who, attempting to live in a world of delusion, is crushed by the reality he evades.

James Joyce's famous collection of stories, *Dubliners*, provides similar examples, manifesting, as a recurring theme, a heartbreaking failure to achieve cherished values (as in the case of Eveline, discussed above). John Steinbeck's "Dustbowl" novels—the widely-read *The Grapes of Wrath* and *Of Mice and Men*—depict the powerlessness and resultant crushed dreams of poor workers suffering under a social system that grants them neither respect nor opportunity.

Such stories and numerous others reveal modernist literature's fundamental principle regarding characterization: Man cannot. The world is not open—reality is not favorable, but inauspicious to human aspiration. Regarding value attainment, it is not a benevolent but a malevolent universe.

Nick Carraway, narrator of F. Scott Fitzgerald's most enduring novel, states perfectly the Modernist conception of man's futile goal pursuit, saying fittingly—at story's finale—of the "great" but doomed Gatsby: "Gatsby believed in the green light, the orgiastic future that year by year recedes before us. It eluded us then, but that's no matter— tomorrow we will run faster, stretch out our arms farther ... And one fine morning—So we beat on, boats against the current, borne back ceaselessly into the past."[51]

The human animal is a condemned creature, destined to perpetually dream, hope, aspire—but perennially, inevitably, irrevocably defeated.

Literary anti-heroes are not pernicious, merely pathetic.

Why, then, given both the practical and inspirational benefit of heroes, is modern culture so permeated with this sad spectacle?

The Intellectual Causes of Anti-Heroism

Many writers accurately point to World War I as a watershed moment in Western history, a seismic event marking a pronounced shift from

19th century optimism to 20th century despair. That the "Great War" was a horrific bloodbath of cataclysmic proportions is not to be doubted.

But a catastrophe—even a man-made one displaying all of humanity's opulent capacity for vicious irrationality—is insufficient, in itself, to alter one's assessment of human nature. A view of man is part of philosophy, of one's thinking regarding fundamentals, and can be revised only by an alteration of one's core convictions and ideals.

Further, the 20th century witnessed not merely war, totalitarianism, and genocide—but also antibiotics, significant other medical advance, increased agricultural harvests, aviation, space travel, computers, the Internet, the spread of freedom and prosperity into the Far East with the rise of the "Asian Tigers," the victory of free nations over two forms of totalitarianism—National Socialism and Communism—above all, certainly in the West, a significant rise in human living standards and life expectancies. Human beings were living longer and healthier lives. Why did not such grand-scale, life-improving events generate a surge of optimism among Western intellectuals?

In reality, historic events, however important, do not constitute the main, driving causation of an individual's (or a society's) worldview. Rather, whether at a level explicit or implicit, grounded in conscious theorizing or in subconscious belief, this is the result of a person's conclusions regarding issues much more fundamental.

An individual's worldview depends on his/her answers to the questions of Philosophy.

What kind of universe do we inhabit—one created by an all-good being, or a world that is eternal—is there a God or is there not? How, by what means, do human beings gain knowledge—by observation-based rationality, by faith in a supernatural dimension, by holding their emotions as self-certifyingly accurate? What is human nature? What is the good? What is the good society? Human beings hold, in some form, answers to these questions. Such answers provide a philosophic framework—whether secular or religious, rational or faith-based, conscious or sub-conscious, true or false—within which world events are construed.

The truth is that, at the time of the Great War, theories of two major thinkers pessimistic regarding modern Western society were on the intellectual rise, and that the horrors of the War served as real-time examples that were adduced in support of these theories.

Marx and Freud are variants of a school of thought known as social determinism. (Although, as will be seen, interpreting Freud in this manner is likely mistaken.)

The philosophy of social determinism, in varying iterations, is both intellectually widespread in the contemporary world, and influential on its view of human nature. To the Modernists, society possesses and deploys immense power, dwarfing that of an individual, and often crushing him/her. The philosophy of Marx is a leading version of such a theory.

The Marxist Cause of Anti-Heroism

According to Marx, under capitalism, a relative handful of wealthy individuals control the economic system, and reduce to both destitution and desperation the vast majority of persons, who are then compelled to work—if at all—on terms of the owners. Such terms are driven by remorseless self-seeking. Profit is both the bottom line and the ruling concern. The plight of the numberless poor is, to the powerful, of little account.

"Let them eat cake," Marie Antoinette mythically replied when informed that the poor had no bread. Whether true or (most likely) apocryphal of the 18th century Queen of France, such dismissive contempt for the downtrodden is—to Marx—indubitably true of modern capitalists.

In *King Lear*, Shakespeare writes: "As flies to wanton boys are we to th' gods. They kill us for their sport." A Marxist paraphrase might read: As flies to wanton boys are laborers to owners. They work us to death for their profit ... and initiate brutal force against us when we seek to organize in support of our rights. The "Dustbowl" novels of Steinbeck are representative literary examples of such philosophy.

Nor, in Marxist theory, is the ruling class's exploitative moral code ameliorable. It is an integral part of an overall philosophy that construes human life in terms of volition, personal initiative, inalienable individual rights, private property, profit, wealth acquisition, and the capacity of a bright, talented, determined person to make his/her own way in the world.

This is the cognitive framework within which the owning class conceptualizes its world; it is immersed in such philosophy; it professes it to its young and promulgates it to its fawning wannabes. Ideas originating outside its class-view are, to it, alien, foreign, inimical. It cannot recognize truth or merit therein.

Consequently, to Marx, a capitalist social system is pernicious in a related form: It seduces uncritical workers with the lure of commercial success and wealth. The American Dream, for example, that, by means of hard work and strong character, a poor individual might rise into middle-class comfort or, beyond, into immense wealth—the Rags to Riches motif—is a conviction deeply entrenched among many native-born Americans, and perhaps, even more so among immigrants.

This theme was central to the works of Horatio Alger, a late-19th century American writer of boys' books, notably *Ragged Dick*, but including numerous others, stressing honesty and work ethic as the dual keys to pronounced upward economic mobility. Alger's books sold millions of copies in his lifetime and the decades subsequent, but his theme, and the American Dream more broadly, is considered—by Marxists—arrant mythology, an unreachable Sirens' call luring unwary members of the lower classes to chase unattainable goals, resulting inevitably in crushing economic and personal frustrations.

Willy Loman is a perfect literary example. He idolizes his older brother, Ben, who appears in the play solely as a figment of Willy's imagination, and who purportedly ventured as a young man into the African jungles and made a fortune in diamonds. Did Ben Loman actually succeed in this manner? It is unclear in the story—but one thing, to Marxists, is certain: Ben is as shadowy to Willy as, in real life, was Andrew Carnegie to millions of destitute laborers and hungry immigrants who futilely sought, during the late-19th and turn-of-the-20th centuries, to emulate his rags-to-riches success story.

The myth, according to Marxists, continues to the current day, sustained by migrant workers, lured to America by promise of higher wages, only to find there oppression and poverty. Arthur Miller, in the play, shows the myth's seductive attraction: Willy's son, Happy, despite the miserable life and suicidal death of Willy, determines to pursue the same unattainable dream as his father.

Happy Loman buys into the capitalist myth and seeks, via diligent work ethic, to reach the commercial dream that lured his father to destruction.

Others turn to crime.

The urban toiling class—according to Marx's intellectual heirs—trapped in dead end jobs and squalid slums, denied access to elite schools and choice careers, will inevitably manifest higher crime rates; for if the capitalist system preaches the creed of wealth but, in action, denies its underclass honest access to it, what other route to the ideal is viable?

Alan Sillitoe's short story of working class defiance, "The Loneliness of the Long-Distance Runner," is a memorable example. Its main character, Smith, a teenage tough from a working class slum, is sent to reform school for petty crime, enlisted to competitive running, but expresses his contempt for the exploitative system by deliberately sabotaging an important race. His planned future crimes represent a challenge to bourgeois power, as much as an illicit means to gain increased wealth.

Marx's philosophy of class struggle and callous exploitation maintains that millions of persons are victims—helpless or defiant—of an oppressively grasping society. A hardened few may be sufficiently ruthless and powerful to bulldoze their way upward into the owning class, trampling along the way their principles and fellow workers, but the rest, the overwhelming preponderance, are condemned to a lifetime of toil for their avaricious masters.

Marxism's widespread influence among the intellectual elite is a primary cause of the dreary anti-hero procession among serious writers.

Another is the interpretation (and probable misinterpretation) by numerous Modernist literary figures of the psychological theories of Freud.

The Freudian Cause of Anti-Heroism

To a significant degree, Freud's psychological work emphasizes, not the power of reason but of unconscious, non-rational, even irrational drives of human behavior.

The intelligent, educated layman, not immersed in study of psychology, might know little of Freud's positive theories of the process, nature, and purported therapeutic benefits of psycho-analysis. But he/she will have some slight familiarity with the clinician's ideas regarding oedipal and electra complexes, a three-part view of human nature composed of id, ego, and superego, the predominance, in human behavior, of psycho-sexual motivations, and a generalized understanding of human beings in terms not of conscious thinking but of unconscious, often repressed and unidentified desires.

Observe in serious literature instances of anti-hero characters of this distinctive variety.

Eugene O'Neill's *Mourning Becomes Electra* is a paradigm example. Set after the termination of the U.S. Civil War, the plot roughly mirrors that of Aeschylus' *Oresteia* trilogy, featuring a returning general murdered by his unfaithful wife—a son who yearns for an incestuous affair with his mother—a daughter fervently devoted to her father, who aspires to supplant her mother as the object of her father's affection, who convinces her brother to kill first the mother's lover, then their mother—and so forth.

Sister and brother are driven to acts of violence not from devotion to the gods or a moral code demanding justice—but from electra and oedipal urges simmering in each one's subconscious. It is a nightmarish, modernist rehashing of Aeschylus as seen through the author's understanding of Freud.

A related outgrowth of Freud's theorizing is a widespread belief in popular culture that families are generally dysfunctional, individuals often neurotic; and that pyscho-pathology, in Western society, is not merely rampant, but of the highest degree of intellectual interest. Mental health, in effect, *or the drive toward it*, is often considered, by modern intellectuals, secondary in significance to its lack—second not only in prevalence, *but in importance.*

William Faulkner, for example, creates a fictitious universe populated by an arresting, eye-popping panoply of neurotics, tormented souls, and psychopaths, each more deeply disturbed than the last. *The Sound And The Fury*, for example, considered one of his finest novels, relates the tale of the Compsons, an aristocratic Mississippi family in the process of egregious decay.

The family is obsessed with the sole daughter, Candace "Caddy" Compson, who rejects Southern values of virtue, feminine virginity, and family honor, engaging in sexually promiscuous behavior. She is divorced by her husband after he discovers that he is not her child's father—and then, disgraced—disowned by her family. She disappears from the area and from the family's purview, departing for Europe. (In a 1945 Appendix to the novel, Faulkner implies that, in Paris during World War II, she becomes the paramour of a Nazi officer.)

Her brother, Quentin, the eldest Compson child, loves his sister, but haunted by Southern conceptions of family honor, becomes paralyzed with despair over her ignominy; suggests to her incest that he might share her punishment; is revolted by the cynical, uncaring response of their alcoholic, fatalistic father; and, as a college student, commits suicide.

Benjy, the youngest Compson child, is mute and severely retarded, therefore another source of disgrace to the family; he cherishes his sister, the only family member who showed him love, and dearly misses her. In his youth, after an assault on a neighbor girl, the family has him castrated.

Jason, the other Compson child, is a scheming, unprincipled black-guard, the favorite of his hypochondriac, self-pitying mother; he is responsible for castrating Benjy and for embezzling the child support money sent to the family by Caddy for her illegitimate daughter, Miss Quentin.

The youthful Miss Quentin, wild and rebellious, steals back her rightful money (and, additionally, Jason's life savings, as well) and absconds with a circus performer, living out the same tormented legacy as her mother.

Not a scintilla of mental health—*or even a desire for it*—is apparent in the members of the Compson family.

Faulkner comes to his view of disturbed man, troubled man, tormented man, not, presumably, from study of Freud; but from experience, at the turn of the 20th century, of the slow rot into degradation and mental ennui of white men whose ancestors, in the Old South—despite the horrors of human slavery—included men of generous nature and moral stature.

But his despair-laden view of man's psychic agony mirrors, in a form specific to the American South, a similar man-view arrived at by other modernist literary figures from their understanding of Freud.

Related, Faulkner was born in 1897, grew up during the early 20th century, and was a brilliant, well-educated mind. *The Sound And The Fury* was published in 1929. Were there Southern writers who expressed such a view of human nature earlier in the post-bellum South—say, in 1889? If not, why not? Granted that geniuses, literary or otherwise, do not arrive on a timetable, like a well-organized railway system, it is nevertheless difficult to conceive of an American novel—prior to

Freud—expressing a view of human nature similar to that dramatized in *The Sound And The Fury.*

And, in 20th and early 21st century serious literature, so it goes. Human individuals are frequently depicted as troubled souls twisted into personal agony by perversely sick and dismayingly powerful families. This form of social determinism—exhibiting individuals buffeted by a dominant social unit—differs markedly from Marx, but a form of social determinism it is.

Questioning the Anti-Hero Philosophy

Human beings are victimized by an oppressive social system or by a dysfunctional family. Man's potential for moral stature, in the modernist worldview, is sorely lacking: The capacity to choose one's goals and means, to rise out of family madness and/or challenge iniquitous society, to nurture one's inner world and thereby effect growth in the outer, to avidly seize opportunities and volitionally shape destiny, to ascend, to achieve, to succeed, to attain abiding joy by winning resplendent victories, to climb, to fly, to soar, to scale heroic heights—such a view of human nature, principally for the reasons described above, is, in the preponderance of the modern literary corpus, sorely lacking.

Faulkner himself succinctly summarized what may be taken as a recurring theme of 20th and early 21st century serious literature: "...I give you the mausoleum of all hope and desire ... I give it to you not that you may remember time, but that you might forget it now and then for a moment and not spend all of your breath trying to conquer it. Because no battle is ever won he said. They are not even fought. The field only reveals to man his own folly and despair, and victory is an illusion of philosophers and fools."[52]

"You are all a lost generation," reputedly observed Gertrude Stein to a young Ernest Hemingway, giving voice to the haunted despair of the 1920s cadre of burgeoning intelligentsia and literary artists.

The Great War had indeed served as a searing, brain-battering example of the pessimistic theories gaining intellectual credibility during the era. Tragically, human history and current events are permeated with gruesome, ongoing instances of man's brutal inhumanity to his brothers and sisters. This is a verity sadly undeniable.

Just as undeniable, however, are the great achievements of the human mind, several of them described in this book. Human beings' capacity to promote prospering life, and the attainments by which they have done so, are just as much part of the historic record as are the atrocities and catastrophes. Goethe's poetry, for example, Beethoven's symphonies, Einstein's physics, and much else of immense value outlived National Socialism. George Washington was as real as Stalin. The bubonic plague horrifically expunged the lives of tens of millions, to be sure; but Louis Pasteur and mankind's improved capacity to effectively treat germ-borne disease are, felicitously, equally true of our heritage.

How will a rational admirer of heroes respond to the profound pessimism embodied in the anti-hero mentality? What are the fundamental points to be made against it? What are its errors?

Errors of the Marxist Foundations of Anti-Heroism

This is not the place to argue the theory of free will versus any form of determinism. Here it will suffice to identify counter-examples showing social determinism to be false. The reasons of its falsity are a topic for another place. (See Appendix B: "A Challenge to Determinism.")

Let us begin with the Marxist premise that the workingman and the poor are inevitably, inexorably ground beneath the booted heel of an oppressive capitalist system.

One important point (of many) to be made against Marxism, and specifically contra the Willy Loman-version of modern anti-heroes, is that the Horatio Alger theme is true and supported by abundant empirical data: Individuals, living under conditions of individual rights and political-economic freedom, often rise from rags to riches—and many more from poverty to middle-class comfort ... and do so, overwhelmingly, by virtue of intelligence and honest effort.

Before referencing a multitude of examples, it is good to make antecedent philosophic points regarding wealth and poverty.

That is, such concepts as "wealth" and "poverty" are as fully relational as are "tall" and "short." The author, for example, is a six-foot man—is he tall or short? Relative to differing others, he is both: Tall relative to a petite woman, short relative to many professional basketball players.

Similarly, the current writer earns roughly $50,000.00 per year teaching Philosophy. Does this make him rich or poor? Again, the question must be asked: Relative to whom? Relative to the many millionaires living in the capitalist and semi-capitalist nations, he is poor; but relative to the masses of semi-starving persons in the pre-capitalist and non-capitalist countries, he enjoys fabulous wealth.

What is considered "middle-class" in America—and all over the semi-capitalist world—is luxury by pre-and-non-capitalist standards. Those, in America, and the semi-capitalist world more broadly, who rise from poverty to middleclass comfort, have indeed, by standards throughout the non-capitalist world, both historically and currently, risen from penury to great wealth.

Honest scan of the historic and contemporary record reveals several important truths: 1. Living standards in pre-capitalist, semi-feudal Europe were, for the vast preponderance of the population, at or near starvation levels. Incomes were generally measured in no more than several hundreds of dollars per year.[53] 2. This same heartbreaking truth still applies across the non-capitalist nations that Mao termed the "3rd World."[54] 3. Over the past century or more, the billions of persons *enjoying middle-class comfort* across the semi-capitalist world in Europe, North America, and Asia—in Hong Kong, Japan, Taiwan, and South Korea—are descendants of persons who clawed their way upward out of abysmal poverty, and did so, overwhelmingly, by means of brain power, honesty, and hard work.

In logic, a culture-wide ascent from starvation-level penury to widespread middle-class affluence is inevitably driven by honest effort, neither by spoliation nor duplicity; for wealth must be produced; before it may be plundered, it must be created; neither chicanery nor rapine will grow crops, design homes or skyscrapers, research and cure disease, or nurture the intellectual advances in science, logic, and rational philosophy upon which such progress is founded. Human beings—many of them—under conditions of political-economic freedom, are working intelligently and productively.[55]

Marx and his heirs argue that capitalism's wealth was gained by exploitation, human slavery, and/or imperialism; in effect, it was plundered.

In answer, let us first remember that wealth is not money; wealth is homes, automobiles, food, medical care, and the like; wealth is goods and services that support human life; money is but an invaluable means of facilitating the exchange of such goods and services, obviating necessity for a primitive barter economy.

Who created the wealth enjoyed in the semi-capitalist nations?

Thomas Edison invented an incandescent electric light and a power station enabling his invention to light parts of New York City; Nikola Tesla, a Serbian immigrant to America, invented an AC induction motor and, together with inventive entrepreneur, George Westinghouse, used alternating current to provide electricity across the vast distances of the North American continent; Alexander Graham Bell invented the telephone, a device that revolutionized communication first in America, then around the globe; Henry Ford's mass production of the automobile revolutionized transportation the way Bell's invention had revolutionized communication; and the Wright brothers' invention of powered flight took that transportation revolution to (literally) new heights. American pharmaceutical companies mass-produced penicillin and later researched, developed, and sold other antibiotics, effective against differing forms of infection, leading to longer lives enjoyed in greater health. Such advances, and numerous others, constitute wealth.

Let's employ an honest question-and-answer method:

From whom were these advances stolen? Nobody. Prior to their invention, from whom could they possibly have been stolen? Nobody. Before their invention, how many persons even dreamed of such goods? Few.

What is, in truth, responsible for such progress? One factor is the individual liberty of American capitalism, enabling independent minds to think as they will, to create new theories and technologies, to require neither governmental nor religious approval, to start entrepreneurial ventures, to seek and gain funding, to compete with older methods and technologies, to demonstrate their innovations to customers, to succeed in business, and to earn a well-deserved fortune.

Further, if imperialism is the driving force of wealth accumulation, why was the Soviet Empire—before it collapsed—abysmally backward, desperately poor, and utterly dependent on the semi-capitalist West for whatever degree of technological advance it begged, borrowed, or stole?[56] Recall that such American achievements were reached at the turn of the 20th century. Why were such advances not created in the Ottoman Empire, which subjugated and controlled Eastern Europe for centuries and lasted into the 20th century? If human slavery is an indispensable cause of wealth creation, why was the American South much poorer than the North? Why did America's wealth-creating Industrial Revolution occur in the North and why, overwhelmingly, after the 13th Amendment ended slavery in 1865? Why were the Soviet Union, Communist China, and Communist Cambodia—all of whom imposed massive slave labor—desperately poor?

The answer: Because imperialism and slavery are conquest, repression, quashing of indigenous freedom fighters, warfare, bloodshed, brutality, tyranny, and suppression of independent thinkers. It is not the cultural and political freedom of the mind upon which such innovations depend. George Washington Carver would have been enslaved under a continuing slave system, denied an education, and most likely forced to work in the cotton fields. Consider the immense difference in both creativity and productivity between Carver the agricultural scientist … and Carver the field hand.

The principle of individual rights made possible, in the capitalist and semi-capitalist nations, history's most impressive and life-enhancing mass migration: That from starvation-level destitution to prosperity undreamed of prior to the 19th century.[57]

Today, Marxists recognize that capitalism creates vastly more intellectual and material wealth than does socialism—but complain that such wealth is unequally distributed.

Observe that the intelligent laymen, judging by their actions, hold sharply differing values than do Marxist intellectuals. The immigration patterns trend heavily toward the capitalist and semi-capitalist nations. By contrast, the more consistently socialist a regime is, the more sedulously it constructs walls, obstacle courses, and machine gun outposts to coercively restrain its citizens from fleeing. To put the point bluntly: Socialists build walls to keep people in. Some who claim to support capitalism want to build walls to keep people out. The intelligent laymen, by the countless hundreds of millions, understand that it is vastly preferable to earn $20,000.00 per annum in a nation where others are millionaires than it is to earn $3,000.00 a year in a nation where others earn the same.

Prosperity, not equality, is a proper economic ideal.

The moral principle of individual rights lays the groundwork for such widespread prosperity—and for extensive upward (and downward) economic and social mobility. It is under a system of individual rights, and only under such a system, that a "rags-to-riches," poverty-to-affluence motif regularly plays out.

As an example, consider the life story of Benjamin Franklin. A full century before Horatio Alger penned uplifting stories of destitute youths who, via pluck and principle, struggled in successful ascent,

Franklin, a blooming writer, scientist, inventor, and statesman, that *ne plus ultra* of American polymaths, lived it out in real time.

A teenage runaway from his Puritan home in Boston, then a struggling printer's apprentice in Philadelphia, eventually so successful a business-man as to enable retirement at age forty-two, in time a protean innovator of the 18th century Enlightenment—one of his many enduring legacies is establishment of a template by means of which a person might consciously direct development of his/her moral character on an upward path.[58]

Franklin writes: "...that it was, therefore, everyone's interest to be virtuous who wished to be happy ... and I should from this circum-stance ... have endeavored to convince young persons that no quali-ties are so likely to make a poor man's fortune as those of *probity* and *integrity*." His autobiography makes clear his socio-economic rise via honesty and industriousness.[59]

If Franklin is a standout example of the penury-to-prosperity prin-ciple, one of his colleagues during America's Revolutionary period—Alexander Hamilton—is even more so.

He was born out of wedlock and impoverished on St. Kitts in the Caribbean. As a youth, he lay in bed, sick of a fever he had contracted from his mother, while she, next to him, died of it, soaked in her own blood, vomit, and urine. Historian, Joseph Ellis writes: "Any attempt to imagine the young Hamilton of that horrific moment as a prominent statesman in a land he had never seen defies credibility."[60]

But budding genius enabled him, as a teenager, to first astonish merchant employers with mastery of accounting, and then to write in a local newspaper vividly, brilliantly of a recent hurricane, impressing the island gentry, who financed his passage to North America, where he might receive an education commensurate with his profuse gifts. Early in 1773, his ship sailed into Boston harbor, from whence he immedi-ately made his way to New York to make his fortune. "It was a perfect match. The prodigy had come to the land of opportunity."[61]

The War of Independence provided the young student a chance to prove himself: The callow youth's courage made him an artillery commander; his ability made him Washington's aide-de-camp; his martial prowess made him a war hero at Yorktown; and his genius enabled him to master finance while waging war. Later, his patriotism made him a father of the Constitution; his writing expertise established him as a lead author of *The Federalist Papers*; and his brilliance as Washington's Treasury Secretary set the country on solid financial foundations. His vision, in time, paved the way for the United States as a germinating urban, industrial, capitalist power.

The bastard son of a disgraced and soon-to-be-dead Caribbean woman—Hamilton's ascent to financial wizard and founding father of U.S. capitalism involves a distance measurable in socio-economic light years.

A list of real-life Horatio Alger stories could be indefinitely extended to fill an encyclopedia.

But take one final, recent example.

Sam Walton, founder of Wal-Mart, wrote an auto-biography, *Made In America*, that sold millions of copies and made various best-seller lists. He was born in Oklahoma in 1918 and went to high school in rural Missouri during the Depression. To help support his poor family, he worked at numerous odd jobs—milking the family cow, bottling the surplus, then driving the milk to customers—he delivered newspapers, sold magazine subscriptions, and, during his college years, waited tables in exchange for meals.

Although he struggled during his early years in business, eventually his innovative methods at Wal-Mart enabled billions of customers to spend less, thereby aiding wealth creation in a form of either increased savings or purchase of other consumer goods. Indeed, his business model proved so popular with customers that, by the mid-1980s, he was listed by *Forbes* magazine as America's wealthiest man, with a net worth of roughly $20 billion.

Additionally, the success of the destitute, hard-working country boy provided inspiration to countless individuals, mired in poverty, but seeking to claw out for themselves and their families a better life.

Where was a John Steinbeck to tell the story of this poor, Depression-era kid? No "Dust Bowl" novel to chronicle the arc of his life? No Hollywood film based on *Made In America*?

It is very sad, but to-be-expected, that in an intellectual culture dominated by an anti-hero mentality, novels and films based on the lives of such heroes as Sam Walton are not forthcoming.[62]

As stated, wealth and poverty are relational concepts. Twenty thousand or thirty thousand dollars per annum in a capitalist or semi-capitalist nation constitutes wealth only dreamed of in the countries where individual rights are repressed—and, in truth, millions, undoubtedly hundreds of millions, perhaps billions of hard-working individuals, including innumerable immigrants to relatively free lands (and their children), have earned annual incomes substantially greater than this.[63]

How extensive is any attempt to compose a full list of the persons that, under individual rights, rose via work ethic and principle from poverty to middleclass affluence? The number is countless, the list expansive, the labor Herculean, the task unachievable.

Regarding the philosophic foundations of literary anti-heroism, previously unmade points can now be established. Claims that the "self-made man" story is chimera are mistaken. This canard has been falsified, in action, under capitalism, on three continents, for two centuries, by millions—perhaps billions—of cases.

The Marxist version of social determinism is flagrantly erroneous.

Heroic stories of self-made men and women are—abundantly—grounded in reality.

Errors of the Freudian Foundations of Anti-Heroism

The anti-hero authors influenced by Marx have, at least, properly understood him. But those influenced by Freud have ignored the positive aspects of the clinician's theories.

In the writings and practice of Freud himself, the purpose of psycho-analysis was to promote a growth from mental illness to mental health. He was a pioneer—and a giant—in the field of clinical psychology.

In reality, in the varied forms of psycho-therapy, including but not limited to Freud's specific variant, do patients gain this latter, superlative value?

Over the past century, an incalculable number of individuals have sought help via differing forms of verbal counseling. Many are honest, conscientious, hard-working, courageous individuals, willing to face painful, perhaps frightening truths about their lives and their families; to make alterations in modes of behavior; to break patterns, to promote growth, to facilitate change, to resolve inner conflict.

Are we to assume that few—or even none—of such patients make significant progress toward enhanced mental health? The facts of the rich and diverse field of psycho-therapy emphatically refute such a judgment. Both popular books written by practicing clinicians—and professional texts and journal articles, intended not for the layman but for colleagues—describe, anonymously, numerous case studies wherein determined patients make positive strides toward elevated health.[64]

Heroes have overcome so much. Are we to believe such magnanimous souls incapable of resolving mental health disorders? Granted that there are combat veterans willing to face enemy machine gun fire but unwilling to face inner "demons," what such truth tells us is not that the demons are fearsomely insuperable, but that there are differing kinds of courage.

Just as strong-willed individuals, possessing the requisite variety of steely fortitude, face and overcome crippling physical disabilities and life-threatening bodily ailments, so some, possessing valor congruent to the menace, face up to and stare down the inner demons. Joanne Greenberg's (*nom de plume*, Hannah Green) brilliant *I Never Promised You a Rose Garden*, for example, is a semi-autobiographical novel depicting a fictionalized account of the author's courageous (and successful) real-life struggle to re-claim greater portions of her mental health.[65]

Related, psychiatrist, Viktor Frankl, in his widely-studied *Man's Search for Meaning,* tells the brutal tale of his capacity to survive Nazi death camps, the form of psycho-therapy—based on it—he devised, and the positive impact it has on patients.[66]

Those individuals wrestling inner demons in successful striving for mental well-being—and/or seeking and discovering meaning in calamity, fueling their inner drive to fulfillment—have chosen genuinely heroic undertakings.

If poor lost souls, irrevocably stunted by monstrously demented families, are worthy of our attention, how much more so are the heroes who refuse to enter the contest of survival wielding solely the hand dealt them, but who, in disdain, fling down the cards, and, in effect, change the game? Such heroes, often with the aid of professional practitioners, make difficult life changes and carve out for themselves positive new rules and peacefully productive modes of being.

Where, in modern literature, are their stories? Who tells the tale of such silent giants? Where are the hero-worshipping authors aching to explore this psychological gold mine of case studies?

There exists but a sad paucity of them.

It is now—early in the 21st century—time to flip on its head the modernist construal of Freud and his descendants in the rich field of psycho-therapy. Do many persons suffer from mental health disorders? Without a doubt. Is it possible for many, even in the absence of counseling, to face up to their demons, and make positive strides toward personal fulfillment—for example, to overcome alcoholism? Indeed— the phenomenon known as going "cold turkey," and those who successfully navigated the arduous process, illustrates this.

Above all, by making the choice to engage in psycho-therapy—by determining to alter old patterns militating against self-realization— can willful individuals progress toward heightened psychological soundness? Innumerable real-life case studies from a multitude of experienced practitioners conclusively establish that they can.

As one example, Irvin Yalom, a distinguished psychiatrist, writing of the advances made in psycho-therapy by a dying patient, stated regarding the expiring man's progress: "...it ... answers for all time the question of whether it is rational or appropriate to strive for 'ambitious' therapy in those who are terminally ill."[67]

Herein lies an estimable goal for twenty-first century novelists: Integrate at least a rudimentary understanding of the principles, practice, and results of psycho-therapy with a confirmed commitment to heroism. After-all, is survival-driven combat with inner monsters no less valorous than that with outer ones? Such tales will produce distinctively modern forms of fiction depicting epic struggles worthy of Homer.

CHAPTER TEN

Hero Worship

We opened this book with a brief discussion of Jack Schaefer's *Shane*. The story is among the best writings, either of fiction or non-fiction, studying the phenomenon of hero worship.

Recall the scene most salient in this regard.

Bobby, in hiding, had been sole witness to the climactic gunfight. He wants to believe in the invincible prowess of his now-wounded hero. "'I don't care,' I said, the tears starting." 'I don't care if he was the fastest that ever was. He'd never have been able to shoot you, would he? You'd have got him straight, wouldn't you—if you had been in practice?'

"He hesitated a moment. He gazed down at me and into me and he knew. He knew what goes on in a boy's mind and what can help him stay clean inside through the muddled, dirtied years of growing up. 'Sure. Sure, Bob. He'd never even have cleared the holster.'"

Observe that Bobby desperately needs to believe that Shane, if in practice, could have dispatched the murderous villains without harm to himself—despite abundant evidence in the story of the villains' formidable capacity.

The boy ardently desires to believe in the power of the good—in its dominance over the evil.

Shane, knowing better than any character in the universe of the story, how demanding is the triumph of good over evil, supports the boy's hopeful belief: The good is not merely powerful; it is perennially commanding. Bobby must believe this claim, so that he may grow to be the man Shane hopes him to become.

But the good, in the story, is represented in two diverse forms: Bobby's father, Joe Starrett—and Shane.

It is perhaps natural that a young boy will idolize the man of virtually superhuman physical prowess, who, in service to the good, stands up to and single-handedly defeats the evil. Shane is, no doubt, a hero.

But is he the right hero for Bobby to emulate?

Clearly, Shane does not think so. He does not want Bobby to grow up to be a gunfighter, no matter how virtuous. He prefers Bobby to grow to be like his dad, a producer, a hard-working farm owner, a man of peaceful nature and of impeccable character.

Therein lies the tale's sad irony. The warrior, in making the valley safe, thereby estranges himself from the peaceful family he loves. That Shane is a great man—and a good man—is not to be doubted. But would you want your daughter to marry a gunfighter? Would you want your son to emulate one? Most parents, given the choice, would understandably prefer Joe Starrett as a match and/or as a role model. Shane agrees. He rides away, thereby reducing his influence on the gestating boy, facilitating hopefully Bobby's emulation of his father.

Nevertheless, the novel is Shane's story. It is about his desire to give up a warrior's life, and create a new existence of peaceful non-violence. It is about his love for the Starrett family—and about the brutal alternative that soon confronts him: Hold to his dream, and let Joe Starrett be murdered—or surrender it, save the people he loves, but lose them in another form.

Joe Starrett is a noble man, an independent man, an authentic hero, but, in this tale, a secondary figure. This is why the story is aptly titled: *Shane*—not *Starrett*. It is Shane, not his father that teaches Bobby the paramount lesson of the story, and perhaps of life:

The good is stronger than the evil.

A hero, regardless his specific field, though he/she be a real life or fictional personage, whether a creator of values, a protector of them—or both—shows that good persons originate life-supporting values, produce them, and, when necessary, effectively defend them.

A hero shows us the efficacy of the good.

To put this point in more philosophic terms, a hero is an exemplar of an important metaphysical truth: The potency of the men and women of virtue, of the men and women devoted to advancing, rather than harming or expunging innocent human life.

Bobby hero worships Shane. Shane wants him to hero worship his father. Which one is right?

The Meaning of Hero Worship

The term, "worship," taken literally, has long been deployed as a religious concept, denoting a moral and emotional state of sublime admiration and awe directed at a supernatural god. Man, in contrast to such an elevated being, is considered diminished, sinful, ignoble.

But the term "worship" need be assigned to neither a mystical dimension nor a man-debasing philosophy. Rather, it can and ought to be construed as a secular, man-glorifying concept. Toward what, if not a supernatural creator, is it directed?

In her "Introduction" to the 25th anniversary edition of *The Fountainhead*, Ayn Rand answered:

"But such concepts—as "sacred," "reverence," "worship"—do name actual emotions, even though no supernatural dimension exists; and these emotions are experienced as uplifting and ennobling.... What, then, is their source or referent in reality? It is the entire emotional realm of man's dedication to a moral ideal."[68]

Presumably, Rand means that when human beings hold a vision of the morally perfected, when they strive conscientiously to reach it, when they yield to no power or obstacle in their path, they achieve an exalted state.

What is the emotional life of such a person? It is one of reverence for the ideal and for those who seek it, oneself included. It is one of uplift, for a noble dedication is ennobling. It is one appropriate to an individual who has devoted his life to the sublime.

The furtherance, in some form, of human life is the noblest ideal. This is, as has been seen, a central aspect of being a hero.

Heroes, by placing their prowess in service of life-sustaining values, and by unflinchingly facing substantial obstacles and/or dangers in so doing, pre-eminently exemplify "man's dedication to a moral ideal."

The character and abilities of several of our major heroes, and the achievements these actuated, constitute an excellent example.

When everyman or everywoman encounter such exalted personages as Montessori and Carver, what is his/her proper moral assessment and response? Should he react with virulent loathing and envious desire to undercut the icons? Ought he merely to yawn with indifference? Respond with a modicum but not an overabundance of respect? Or perhaps, he should recognize superlative human stature and render due homage to the sublime?

The latter is the attitude of hero worship. To contemplate a hero's life should, properly, be an act of worship.

Such an act of hero worship, directed toward one worthy of it, is a profoundly virtuous action—one of justice and of commitment to thriving human life. The action benefits everybody. Epic heroes, such as Montessori and Carver, have earned such homage; and, in sincerely paying it, a hero worshiper experiences the highest emotions of which man is capable: A sense of the exalted.

To contemplate the sublime, to revere it, fills one's spiritual life with visions of the upright and the great, with an admiring love of the truly sacred: Human beings at their noblest and life-giving best.

The human soul—intellect, character, and emotions—has a capacity to seek, discover, and venerate the sublime. The inward experience of hero worship is a good in itself, requiring neither an ulterior reason to justify it nor a further end to which it provides means. Although the experience may lead to no further action or event, one's life is immensely richer for it.

Nevertheless, hero worshipers can do more.

Hero Emulation

Many superlatively good things can properly be desired as ends in themselves—education as an example. The acts of knowing, of understanding complex phenomena, of dispelling ignorance and confusion, bring immense satisfaction into the inner life of a well-educated person. He need carry it no further to gain great value.

But he can choose to.

He might choose, for example, to educate others, a substantial value to human well-being.

Or he might choose to use his knowledge to create wealth. Aristotle, for example, tells the story of how Thales—a scientist and mathematician, and widely held to be the first philosopher—not content to merely know a good deal about astronomy, put his knowledge into lucrative practice: He predicted a bumper crop of olives and, during the ensuing winter, rented all the olive presses. When his prediction came true, many businessmen vied to rent his presses, he charged a high price, and thereby gained a substantial amount of money.

Great things can sometimes be made greater—and something valuable for its own sake can, nevertheless, be deployed to gain a further value. This truth applies to hero worship as well as to knowledge.

A human being is an integrated sum of mind and body. If an individual comprehends a profound truth and/or experiences an uplifting emotion, this is outstanding.

But, additionally, what if the hero worshiper puts the profound truth into practice? What if he/she permits himself to be motivated by the ennobling experience to act more nobly?

Practical deeds impelled by our most insightful acts of consciousness will, in many cases, lead to salutary results.

Hero worshipers can choose also to emulate them.

They can be inspired by heroes to put into practice a similar devotion to life-supporting principles. A hero worshiper, when confronted by a daunting challenge, can ask himself/herself: What would

Shackleton (or another champion) do in this instance? Presumably, a hero's undeterred determination motivates such a hero worshiper to take amelioratory steps in his/her own life.

When an individual, under such circumstances and for such reasons, takes positive steps in his/her own life, then heroes do far more than provide ample portions of emotional exaltation. That exaltation may be used by the worshipers to fuel the taking of remedial action.

Heroes Set an Example

If the good, properly conceived, lies in active promotion of prospering human life, then emulation of genuine heroes benefits everyman and everywoman substantially.

For heroes, in demonstrating the human potential, show how much is possible—and possible to all human beings. For example, one need not be a black woman to be motivated by the story of Sarah Breedlove (Madame C.J. Walker).

Her story virtually defies credibility—born to former slaves in 1867 Louisiana, orphaned at age seven, married at fourteen, a mother at seventeen, widowed at twenty—a single black mother in the segregated south, coercively denied numerous educational and career opportunities—working as a washerwoman for roughly one dollar a day but determined her daughter would receive an education—what were her chances, if estimated during these early years of her life, to become the world's first self-made female millionaire of any race?[69] Low in the extreme.

She defied extraordinary odds and overcame seemingly insuperable obstacles to reach brilliant success as an entrepreneur in the field of woman's beauty care.

She, a human being, accomplished this. People learning her story, regardless of race and gender, are likewise human beings. She shows us—Asian males, for example, or white males, or black women, or any-body—that a human being, coming from origins socially low and from a persecuted racial minority, can (in at least a semi-free society) reach superlatively life-giving achievements.

Sarah Breedlove accomplished much more than creation of outstanding beauty products for black women. Additionally, her story, to any rational hero worshiper, motivates one to set goals high, to demand of oneself the best, in effect, to become the hero of one's own life.[70]

For those among everyman who yearn to live and to achieve fulsomely, her story shows that impediments seemingly insuperable are to be faced head-on, thereby illustrating Shackleton's insight that "difficulties are just things to overcome."

A hero's demonstrated capacity to carry to successful resolution tasks severely problematic shows everyman and everywoman that confidence in his/her ability to attain goals both elevated and demanding is not hopelessly misplaced.

A dauntless spirit to face intractable problems and/or concerted opposition standing in the path of value achievement—this is what hero worshipers observe when contemplating a hero's life. It is what they can achieve if they permit themselves to be inspired by it.

Whether Bobby Starrett continues to hero worship Shane, or shifts focus to his father, or hero worships both, he will gain this priceless value.

Differences in Level of Ability Irrelevant to Hero Emulation

In response to such exalted illustrations, a hero worshiper might be confronted by the following retort: "The hero," it will be said, "presumably possesses prowess substantially greater than everyman—and what is possible to a Sarah Breedlove, an Ernest Shackleton, a George Washington may well exceed the limitations of myriad others."

In facing such a claim, a healthy hero worshiper, as any rational individual, acknowledges facts, even those unpleasant, painful, or frightening; he/she neither ignores nor denies them.

He will recognize in many cases that an epic hero's level of ability does indeed significantly surpass his own. Carver and Montessori, for example, might possess ampler portions of genius; Shackleton and Washington, bodily constitutions more vitally robust; Sarah Breedlove, business acumen exceeding that of a more pedestrian talent; and so forth.

But such hero-worshiping individuals acknowledge a constellation of other truths also germane in this context: That they themselves possesses some level of ability; that such capacity, via unstinting practice, might be nurtured and significantly enhanced; and that a hero's unquailing devotion to values is a moral characteristic—not innately hard-wired but volitionally chosen—and one that might be emulated, replicated, and matched.

Further, while true that a proper hero worshiper might lack an epic hero's surpassing prowess, neither does he/she, in all likelihood, face world-threatening challenges. Unlike George Washington, for example, he seeks neither to militarily defeat the world's mightiest empire nor help found a nation. He/she might seek, rather, to work his way through college, or to lovingly and effectively, as a single parent, rear a healthy, fulfilled child, or to carry to successful fruition a demanding entrepreneurial venture, or perform some other productive endeavor commensurate with the level of capacity possessed.

Of central importance, a rational hero worshiper seeks to (and can) equal a hero's unflinching dedication to values.

The recurring questions posed to self by such individuals are: How would this (greatly admired) hero respond to an intimidating obstacle in my life? After-all, even in absence of the epic hero's degree of prowess, why cannot I respond with the dauntlessness and devotion to human life that a hero does?

Why cannot I respond with the dauntlessness and devotion to human life that a hero does?

Why not, indeed? The answer, of course, is that a hero worshiper can.

This or something like it is the form in which proper hero worshipers might employ a hero's stature to ameliorate their own lives. They understand that, within the scale of their values, concerns, and abilities, they can respond to pressure and/or hardship and/or danger with a commitment to life-enhancing values identical to that displayed by their favored heroes.

In so doing, a hero worshiper substantially maximizes his/her own life opportunities and chances at self-actualization.

Bobby Starrett, if he hero worships Shane, his father, or both, will derive courage to face impediments lying athwart his path to positive value achievement. This is true regardless the profession he selects; for hero worship, fully implemented, does not necessitate mimicking the hero's specific career choice, style of dress, cool Brooklyn accent, or the like.

It necessitates cultivating a spirit sufficiently dauntless to follow one's own conscience.

What Hero Worship is Not

Some who profess to hero worship maintain that everyman and everywoman should grant to the epic hero unquestioning obedience. The idea is that a great hero, being a moral and/or intellectual paragon, will guide everyman's life more benignly than could everyman himself.

There are multiple problems with this belief. To here limit ourselves to the most salient: In many cases, part of what makes an epic hero morally salutary is the courage of his/her convictions, a refusal to surrender his judgment to blindly obey authority. Think of Socrates, think of Maria Montessori, think of Frederick Douglass, think of many others who opposed the secular and/or the religious authority, or who stood tall against the social biases of their day and said, "No, I thank you." Often, part of a hero's character lies in autonomy of thought and functioning, neither in obedience to authority nor conformity to social prejudice.

Should hero worshipers, in action, renounce one of the faculties that made their champion a hero in the first place? Should they perform reverse alchemy, transmuting spiritual gold into lead and heroes who rejected servile obedience into villains who demand it? Should we, to deploy a literary example, truckle abjectly before the Cardinal rather than, a la Cyrano, stand upright on our own principles and refuse the power broker's demand to compromise with our soul?

One grand benefit of hero worship is to live more heroically. It is to emulate the epic hero.

One does not emulate by repudiating a salient characteristic of the one emulated.

Afterword

This slender volume has covered substantial ground.

It has established a hero's nature and identified a cognitive method by means of which epic heroes are distinguished from differing types of non-heroes. It has shown the manner in which the best of everyman and everywoman can rise to heroic stature. It has demonstrated that heroes are exemplars of value-laden, self-fulfilling actions—and that they eschew value-surrendering, self-sacrificing ones. It has argued that grand achievers sometimes have moral flaws, and that such do not necessarily disqualify them from entree into the pantheon of heroes. The book has dissected the phenomenon of literary anti-heroism, showing that, how, and why its underlying premises are false. Finally, it has demonstrated the profound benefits of hero worship, properly understood.

Will this be sufficient, in the 21ˢᵗ century, to incite whole new generations of epic heroes? To encourage the moral best of everyman and everywoman to rise to heroic heights? To rekindle, on a culture-wide scale, the spirit of hero worship?

Prior to the 20ᵗʰ century, serious thinkers generally admired heroes. But two elements were absent from their understanding: 1. A fact-based, inductively-established definition of "hero" 2. An accurate comprehension of hero worship—of what it is and of what it is not. These two have now been provided.

This book does not purport to be an exhaustive analysis of a hero's nature. Presumably, there is more to be said. But it is a provocative first step toward understanding the nature of heroes, one that will hopefully spark a lively 21st century debate regarding this important subject.

It is the writer's sincere hope that future thinkers recognize the nature of heroes and that humanity, once again, deeply, widely, and sincerely celebrates their life-giving exploits.

If these changes come to pass, then this book will have done a great deal of good.

Human Life as the Standard of Moral Value

The question of what makes something good or bad has puzzled philosophers for centuries. For example, if it were said that an individual should work hard and support himself by honest effort, most people would undoubtedly agree. But what makes it good? Is it good because God commands it? Or good because society deems it so? Or good because an individual judges it right for himself? Or, alternatively, is there some fundamental fact of reality that requires it of human beings—that mandates it as a necessity of human life?

Ayn Rand answered this question.[71]

She identified, after 2,500 years of Western philosophy, a rational, fact-based standard of moral value. Prior to Rand, philosophers had often repudiated the idea that values could be based on or derived from facts. For example, David Hume asked the question whether an "ought" proposition can be derived from an "is" proposition—and answered with a resounding "no."

Hume held, in effect, that while he could observe an individual working long hours, earning money, paying bills, devising a budget, putting money in the bank, and so forth—he could not discern the "good" in this. Where is the "good?" he asked. One cannot directly observe it—cannot touch or see or taste it. If there is no observational evidence to establish some action as good, then the good is not based in facts. Hume concluded that no identifiable positive relationship exists between values and facts. Value judgments are not based on the facts of reality—but on some other consideration.

The idea that values cannot be grounded in observable fact, but must be based on something else, has been prevalent in philosophy for millennia—and still is. There are three dominant schools of thought on this issue: the religious, the social, and the personal.

Major Schools of Thought Regarding the Source of Right and Wrong

The religious school holds that God's will is the standard of right and wrong. On this view, anything God commands ... is good by virtue of His will alone. So, for example, if He chooses to flood the earth, killing untold numbers of human beings—or to slay thousands of Hebrews for the crime of worshipping a golden calf—or to permit Satan, on a bet, to torment the virtuous Job—then these actions are good simply because He chose them. An action—any action—is good because God says so. This was the dominant moral theory of medieval Europe and is that of most of today's Middle East.

The social school maintains that society's collective judgment is the standard of right and wrong. On this view, often known as "cultural relativism," good and evil are created by the group, and are relative from one society to another. If, for example, a secular society repudiates God and claims an alternative source of moral law, then, in that culture, moral law legitimately proceeds from this other source; however, if a religious culture judges God to be morality's provider, then, in that society, He properly is.

Similarly, if National Socialists (Nazis) or Communists hold that a man's life belongs to the state, then, in their societies, it properly does;

if the Americans claim that an individual's life belongs to him, then, in America, it rightfully does.

Today, it is common to hear Western proponents of the social school claim, in brutal consistency, that the suppression of women in the Arab-Islamic world—and elsewhere—cannot be condemned, because "it is their culture." This theory is dominant in the modern Western world. In its most consistently virulent form, this was the school of thought underlying and giving rise to both National Socialism and Communism—whose shared precepts include the all-powerful, infallible nature of the State, the State as sole creator of right and wrong, and the non-negotiable obligation of each individual to unquestioningly obey.

If the Aryan state deems it morally right to annihilate 5.1 million Jews (and millions of other "racially inferior" human beings), then, for it, it is so. Similarly, if a Communist "Workers' State" holds it morally proper to exterminate the bourgeoisie as a class, then, in that nation, mass murder of the middle class is ethically upright.

Because society is held akin to a mini-God on earth, this code is merely a secularization of the religious school.

The personal school holds that an individual's sheer will is the standard of right and wrong (for him). Whatever the individual wants to do is good for him—because he wants to do it. "If it feels good, do it" was the refrain of the 1960s hippie movement, giving perfect expression to this code. On the personal code, an individual's feelings tell him the proper actions to perform or shun. If he wants to use toxic drugs, or to engage in indiscriminate sex, or to work productively, or to sponge off of others—or to assault them—or whatever, then doing so is good for him.

"I am higher than you people," wrote Columbine killer, Eric Harris, in his journal. "If you disagree, I would shoot you."[72] Whatever an individual feels or believes—no matter if murderously violent—is right for him ... and right for him to act on.

In the modern Western world, this code is secondary in influence only to the social school. Indeed it is merely a variation on that theory, for, in both, right and wrong are decided subjectively, by whim—whether the individual's or the collective's.

Historically, the choices often offered mankind have been: Follow God's will, follow society's arbitrary dictates, or follow your own whims. What do these three moral codes share in common? Morality has no basis in fact, in nature, in objective reality. Rather, it is decided by the will or whim of some consciousness or group of them.

The Theory That Morality is Objective

It remained for Ayn Rand, in her novel, *Atlas Shrugged*, and in her non-fiction book, *The Virtue of Selfishness*, to demonstrate that objective facts, not subjective whims, form the basis of moral judgments. Rand provided a revolutionary approach to the "ought-is" question. Rejecting the premise that values are grounded in mere desires of some subject(s), she asks the question: What is the fundamental fact of reality that gives rise to the entire phenomenon of valuing?

Once the question is posed in this innovative manner, it points in the direction of the answer: It is only because living beings must attain certain ends in order to sustain their lives that the phenomenon of valuing arises. A living being's values are those things that its nature requires for its survival. An organism's nature is not a matter of whim—but solely of hard, observable fact.

Observe the causal connection between an organism's life and its values. A plant, for example, must gain the water, sunlight, and chemical nutrients that its life requires, without which it will die. Similarly, an animal must find the food and shelter from the elements upon which its life depends; if it fails, it perishes. In the same way, human beings must produce the material necessities of their survival—food, housing, medical care, as three major examples—a creative activity requiring the use of reason. For man, as well, the alternative is stark: Attain specific goals—or perish. In every case, an organism's nature—the factual requirements of its survival—is the source of its values; in no case, is valuing a product of whim or caprice.

"In a lifeless world, there would be no values: no good, no evil. After all, good or evil to whom, and for what? If we grind a rock ... to dust, what has it lost that it previously strove to maintain? Nothing. A rock takes no steps to maintain its rock form as distinct from a pile of dust particles.... Living organisms, on the other hand, engage in processes to sustain their lives. Plants, for example, grow their leaves toward the sun to engage in photosynthesis to support their lives. If we kill the plant, it has lost something that it took steps to sustain—its life. The particular form or shape of a rock is of no value to the rock, nor is the rock's existence of value to it. But an organism's life is of value to the organism—and its life is the precondition and the ultimate goal of all of its other values."[73]

This insight—that the factual necessities of life are the source and origin of valuing—is the indispensable identification that serves as the foundation of a rational ethics.

If a being's life is the source and goal of valuing, then man's life—the life proper to a rational being—must be the standard of moral value. As Ayn Rand states, "that which is proper to the life of a rational being is the good; that which negates, opposes or destroys it is the evil."[74] If the concepts of "good" and "evil" arise solely because certain courses of action promote man's life, and others harm or destroy it, then the good is that which benefits human life—and the evil is that which is inimical to it. "The validation of value judgments is to be achieved by reference to the facts of reality," says Ayn Rand. "The fact that a living entity *is*, determines what it *ought* to do."[75]

Human life is the standard of moral value: Heroes understand this principle, even if only in some unstated, implicit form; and, in the actions that make them heroes, they act on it.

A Challenge to Determinism

In human life, there is no escaping choice.

The alternatives confronting an individual within his/her purview are numerous, often significant, and at times, weightily consequential. For example, a teenager approaches the end of high school. Will he/she attend college? If so, which one? If so, what subject will he specialize in? If not, what will he do? What kind of career does he want? Does he/she seek to marry? If so, will he (and spouse) bring children into the world? Individuals face such important life decisions, as well as a host of lesser issues, on a regular basis. They must choose between and among them—and their choices bear consequences.

That they have the capacity to choose freely among such alternatives, rather than being necessitated by an external agency (or one unknown to their awareness) to select one over another, is validated by direct introspective awareness. An individual, for example, who is fascinated by the Humanities, may need to choose, as a college major, between literature, history, and philosophy. By focusing his/her attention on his own mental processes, he is aware of weighing alternatives, of applying whatever criteria of value he holds, of judging, and of selecting one discipline over the others.

This is equally true of all alternatives faced by a human being, whether of momentous, intermediate, or trivial consequence to his/

her life. Whether mulling a travel route, a diet, a career switch, any or all of the above, or another, the process remains identical: The environment provides a range of alternatives, an individual must choose among them, and introspection reveals a process of willing, voluntary, uncoerced selection.

Take a differing example. It is, let us say, several hours before bedtime. The writer is an inveterate bookworm but, also, an avid sports fan. How will he spend his time? Volume XI, "The Age of Napoleon," of Will Durant's magisterial *The Story of Civilization* lies open on his desk. But there is an NBA playoff game on TV—the highest caliber of basketball in the world. Additionally, he has long been possessed of a secret, perhaps shameful desire to study math. He has purchased the books. Now would be an opportune moment. He is alone in his apartment; no one else is present to observe his guilty indulgence. What to do?

He focuses cognitive attention on his mental processes. He thinks: The spring semester will soon conclude; teaching responsibilities will abate and free time will abound; the later rounds of the NBA playoffs will be eminently accessible. Further: Study of math might be best left to summer vacation, rapidly approaching, when sundrenched moments and extended days may compensate for such a dark habit. He notices that his thought processes continue: History—his story—the study of mankind's past, constitutes must-know truths for any Humanities lover; which the writer emphatically is. This is what he loves; the tug of emotional appeal is strong; there is a pronounced preference to spend these hours with Durant.

He is introspectively aware as he selects study of history—for this specified time period—from amongst a range of possible alternatives. He is conscious of eschewing the other options. He is aware of choosing one over the others.

Epistemologically, if we are to credit the immediate apprehensions of direct awareness, then we must do so comprehensively. Just as our five senses provide immediate awareness of extrospective material objects, just as our nervous system provides vividly immediate bodily sensations, just so, introspection reveals an expansive panoply of thoughts, value judgments, and emotions. On what ground can the reality of any of these apprehensions be doubted?

What basis, for example, is there to doubt the accuracy of my visual awareness regarding automobiles, trucks, pedestrians, and street signs—one means enabling safe driving of my automobile? Similarly, based on what would I doubt the reality of severe bodily pain or tooth-ache, sensations leading me to seek medical or dental remediation?

The exact question applies to introspection: On what grounds can the reality of my thoughts regarding a Presidential election be questioned? What, for example, would count as evidence supporting the claim, "Bernstein's argument against the candidates of both prominent political parties is unreal"? A critic supporting one or another candidate might, with evidence, construct an argument claiming that my conclusion is *mistaken*. But unreal? Nothing could count as evidence for such a claim; for anything understood as evidence would itself be a mental item—and so, subject to the same charge of unreality.

This line of argumentation can be extensively pursued, but the conclusion is and must be: The inner world of thoughts and values is as real as the outer world of entities. Mental activities—such as thinking—are as fully part of the world as are bodily activities. Introspection is as valid a means of awareness as is extrospection.

The reality of choice is known via direct introspective awareness. It is a directly experienced aspect of human consciousness, as real as our thoughts, value judgments, and emotions; as real as our bodily sensations; as real as our auditory perception of music; as real as our visual observation of a truck hurtling down the boulevard.

Rationally, this is the only validation free will requires. For "rational" means showing the basis of x in fact, in reality, in direct awareness.

But, regarding this issue, philosophers have made critical errors; their influential theories require refutation. Unfortunately, much of what needs to be said regarding free will is polemics.

The denial of free will, in various forms, is known as determinism. This theory, in any version, claims that some agency beyond our control and, perhaps, our awareness necessitates our actions, which we do not voluntarily choose.

Expressed in other terms, determinism is the claim that, given the laws of nature and given the facts of history, there is only one possible future. What will be, must be; there is no alternative. This is true of all occurrences, the determinist argues, including human actions. Belief in human free will, therefore, is an error, even an illusion.

Two leading variants are biological determinism and social determinism.

The biological version argues that an individual's thoughts, values, character, and actions are necessitated by his/her internal bodily chemistry—by genetic coding, by neural activity, by the physical laws governing the motion of atoms composing our bodies, and the like.

The social version claims, rather, that it is a person's social "conditioning"—his/her family upbringing, education, social mores, a country's political and legal system, and such things—that make him who and what he becomes.

Let us examine these theories one at a time.

The Errors of Biological Determinism

In truth, certain types of neural firings, electrical discharges of the nervous system, and other biologic functions are a necessary condition of consciousness, human or otherwise. Some persons, by contrast, claim there exist spirits or consciousnesses independent of bodies—that is, ghosts. Is there any un-debunked observable data supporting such a claim? Not that the writer is aware of. Based on best available evidence, the conclusion is that consciousness, all consciousness, including human rational consciousness, inheres within and depends upon a specific type of living body. Biologic activity is a necessary, although not sufficient condition of consciousness.

Do the neural firings or swirling atoms composing our bodies render unreal human free will? How would a necessary condition of consciousness invalidate any of its activities? Rather, does not such bodily activity make them possible? If we expunge such bodily activity, we necessarily efface consciousness and its functions. But if we restore these biologic processes, we empower consciousness and its capabilities.

It is similar regarding claims of quantum physics. Whatever does or does not occur at the sub-atomic level regarding the human brain, nervous system, and body more generally, such activities are a necessary condition of human consciousness. These are requirements for the phenomena of thoughts, values, emotions, and awareness. Physical activities, whether at the macroscopic or microscopic levels, that are necessary for the existence and functions of consciousness, are not disqualifying elements of the very phenomena to which they give rise.

One no more invalidates the reality of free will by explaining the neurological processes that enable both a person's choice and his/her introspective awareness of it—than one invalidates the reality of physical entities by explaining the neurological processes that enable an individual's extrospective awareness of them. Specific forms of brain functions enable the process of awareness; their explanations do not invalidate its content. Or, alternatively phrased, brain activity is a means of consciousness, not a means of disproving the existents of which it is conscious.

Genetic science may well establish that an individual is born with specific predispositions; for example, let us say, a tendency toward alcoholism. What does this actually mean? Does it mean that, physiologically, he/she experiences intense pleasure from consumption of alcohol? Related, does it mean that the physical concomitant of desire for alcohol—some form of brain activity, for example—is unusually well-developed in this person and that it is easily activated?

One thing it does not mean is that such a tendency necessitates this individual taking a first drink. Such a person might accept a drink or refuse it, as innumerable recovering or recovered alcoholics can attest. An individual does not relinquish the capacity to choose between x and non-x by virtue of possessing a genetic predisposition toward x. If, colloquially, such a predisposition is referred to as a biologic "push" toward x, the individual can and often does "push" back.

Going further, even if an "alcoholic" chooses to take a fateful first drink, plunging himself back into the addiction's powerful grip, is it plausible to believe that he is now incapable of refusing a next drink? If, by some fanciful construct, a next drink wrought death for his beloved daughter and refusal to so much as sip alcohol for the next week or month entailed the child's deliverance, will the determinist insist that the alcoholic is necessitated to take the next drink, and that it is *impossible* for him to refuse? When discussed in terms of such momentous personal values, it becomes clear that an "alcoholic" can and, under such conditions, most likely would refuse the next drink.

What type of evidence might a determinist adduce to support his conclusion that an individual did not choose a value of great importance to him?

For example, to effectively argue against the claim that a person chose his career, one must demonstrate that a causal factor independent of the individual's will necessitated, for him, that career—and further explain the means by which that causal factor, or another, inevitably and inescapably entailed his awareness of choice, an awareness thereby shown to be illusory.

Among the other problems of biological determinism, this means that the bodily causes (or necessary conditions) of consciousness ineluctably create a vast illusion suffered perhaps by all members of the human species. How would the physical processes of nervous system and brain—aspects of reality—necessarily, unavoidably, consistently, and perhaps universally create a powerful experience utterly at variance with reality? Where and what necessitates such a sharp break between reality and unreality?

Related, there exists what may be designated: A Challenge to Determinism, of determinism in any form, of determinism as such. The essence of determinism, in any of its iterations—that by virtue of which any view is deterministic—is the claim that some agency not subject to an individual's consciousness or will—be it God, or one's genes, or the laws of physics, or another—controls an individual's actions.

The challenge can be simply stated: What is the conduit by means of which the controlling factor—call it x—controls a person's decision-making and actions? An explanation of a phenomenon involves identification and explication of its cause. For example, regarding the link between cigarette smoking and lung disease, it was insufficient to simply establish a strong empirical correlation; the causal factor—be it the tar, or nicotine, or whatever—must be isolated, and its deleterious effect on living human tissue clinically demonstrated. When researchers repeatedly expose healthy living tissue to a chemical agent and, consistently, that agent promotes cellular degradation, cellular breakdown, and cellular death, a causal relationship is established.

The same principle applies to determinism: The onus of proof is on its supporters to explain and demonstrate two points: (a) The nature of x and *the specific means* by which it causes particular human actions—the actual conduit between x and Ted's action, for example, of proposing to Nancy. (b) That, how, and why the specific functions of x (or another causal agent) create, indeed necessitate, the wide-spread—perhaps universal—experience of free will. The determinist must demonstrate, step-by-step, the causal chain between x and *both* a person's action *and* his/her experience that he chose the action from a range of alternatives, the others of which he volitionally repudiated.

To say, for example, that a human being is a collection of atoms, that atoms operate in strict accordance with physical law, and that, therefore, human beings operate in strict accordance with physical law, is to express a sweeping abstract hypothesis yet devoid of causal explanation. The question remains: How, by what specific processes and steps, does physical law impel me to pen a defense of free will?

Providing a detailed, step-by-step answer to this question is the primary component of any theory seeking to prove the truth of determinism.

A final issue regarding this theory: Determinists have interpreted the research of neurologist/physiologist, Benjamin Libet, in a way that denies human free will. Libet, building on the work of prior researchers, performed a series of experiments showing that, several hundred milliseconds prior to experiencing conscious awareness of a decision to physically move, a human subject underwent brain activity that made possible the move.

More precisely, Libet found that conscious awareness of a decision to move preceded motion by roughly 200 milliseconds; but unconscious activity—electrical potential in the brain—preceded motion by about 550 milliseconds. To determinists, this electrical impulse—a so-called "readiness potential" or RP—is to be construed in several forms: It is the cause of conscious awareness of a decision to move— and/or the cause of the movement itself. Further, to them, it might be that conscious awareness of a decision to move is merely an incidental by-product of the RP, which itself is the sole cause of the motion.

But, in truth, any and all such interpretations of Libet's findings are erroneous.

The first point to remember is that the human mind is far more than conscious awareness; it is, as well, a vast subconscious reservoir. Examples of this deep reservoir abound. For one, I have studied the history of religion at some length and possess a good deal of knowledge regarding it. But, at times, my conscious mind focuses on the free will-determinism issue: My knowledge of the Catholic Church's brutal 13th century suppression of the Albigensian "heresy" (and of much else in the history of religion) is not then in full focal awareness—but can be summoned, on command, into such awareness.

Related: I have numerous childhood memories of playing baseball with my buddies in the park, of watching on television as the Yankees beat the Cincinnati Reds in the 1961 World Series, of going to the beach with my father, and many others that are not, on numerous occasions, in conscious awareness but that could momentarily be recalled.

One final illustration of many that could be offered is my love of my daughter. She is at school as I write this—for this period of time, I am thinking generally about philosophic issues, not anything else—but if I stop for a moment and think of her, or even better, when I see her, the emotion of love surges to the forefront of awareness and submerges all else.

The subconscious mind is rich.

How does it relate to a proper interpretation of Libet's findings? Let us start with an example.

I am working at the computer in my office at home, let us say. It is Saturday morning and, as I work, I am drinking from a bottle of water at my side. After a few hours, I am aware of several issues: One is that I need to use the lavatory—another is that I will soon be hungry and will desire to eat lunch—a third is that I promised to call my daughter before noon. It is now eleven a.m., and I am engrossed in the work, so—for some unspecified period of time, but for fewer than sixty minutes—I put off taking action on these matters.

My conscious mind is focused on philosophic issues. I am not consciously thinking about these other, practical concerns. But my subconscious mind is aware of them and knows that, soon, I will take action on any one or all of them.

Is the RP for these actions sparking in my brain? This is a question for neurologists, not philosophers, to answer. As pure speculation, my guess is that the answer is: Yes. The brain is in a state of preparedness to initiate physical action.

One conclusion from this line of thought is that I could contemplate rising from the chair right now to perform any or all of the deeds mentioned above—the RP for such activity presumably ignites in my brain—and then decide to postpone the activity until a future moment.

I am prepared to take these actions but not right at this moment. I could act at any time, and will act at some. The RP has me in a state of physical-action-readiness but, in and of itself, does not determine the exact moment at which such action is initiated.

Observe that Libet's experiments measured *only for such occasions on which physical activity took place*, the milliseconds between brain preparedness, a conscious decision to act, and the resulting action. He did not measure such temporal relations for occasions *when no action took place*. Libet himself realized that, at times, the RP was operative but no physical action resulted.[76]

The RP, therefore, is not a cause of motion; it is rather a potential for motion—the brain is prepared—but awaits a mental command, whether conscious or subconscious, to move.

Further, how would electrical discharges in the brain and nervous system, or any physical processes independent of consciousness, know: the configuration of my apartment, the location of my lavatory, the foodstuffs in my refrigerator, my daughter's name, address, phone number, interests, values, or anything else regarding her, including my love? Independent of consciousness, the physical processes of brain and nervous system have no more knowledge of such things than do streaks of lightning flaring across a summer sky. The electrical discharges, in and of themselves, could not know to move me toward the phone to call my daughter rather than toward the window to check the weather.

But these specific physical processes make possible consciousness, which can and does understand such matters, which can and does choose to take actions and the time to do so.

Additionally, such minor actions are enormously secondary in human life. What about regarding much more momentous events? Will the determinist claim that Ted proposed to Nancy because, milliseconds before he popped the question, his neurons flickered in a certain manner? Is this really the basis on which men generally propose to their girlfriends?

Or, rather, did Ted propose (and men generally) because he and Nancy had been dating for several years, they held shared values and interests—possibly similar philosophic, religious, and/or political allegiances—they conversed comfortably on a wide range of issues, they took pleasure in each other's company, they enjoyed a genuine intimacy and sexual attraction, they trusted each other's character, and so forth? Presumably, it is for these reasons that he contemplates proposing to her—and for these reasons that his neurons ignite, making possible this specific speech act.

The truth most likely is that Ted had mulled for some time this matter of central importance to his life. There might have been moments when the neurons that make possible speech flickered in his brain, providing readiness to ask the question—but, for various possible reasons, he decided the moment was not right and, so, forestalled taking speech action.

A mere state of preparedness to act is not identical to a cause of action. The determinist interpretation of Libet's research is an example of the logical fallacy of False Cause: Just because event A precedes event B in time does not necessarily mean that event A is the cause of event B.

Indeed, supporters of free will should welcome Libet's findings and deploy them as part of their argument. For Libet's research has accomplished two tasks: 1. It has identified the brain activity that makes possible the choice to physically move 2. It has shown that such brain activity is a potential for physical motion, not a necessitating cause of it. It has shown that a certain kind of brain activity is a necessary condition of physical motion—but not a sufficient condition.

The Errors of Social Determinism

Additionally, to the determinist view must be contrasted stories of numerous individuals who, to significant degree, repudiate much of society's influence, choosing instead to contravene it. How many individuals, for example, reared under Communist totalitarianism, indoctrinated regarding the evils of capitalism and moral superiority of socialism, eschewed it, espoused its converse, and risked their lives to escape to the semi-capitalist West?

How many children of faith-based zealots, in their adult years—or earlier—threw off their religious training to adopt unqualified secularism? Related, how many persons imbued from infancy with the glories of one faith subsequently converted to another—doing so, in some eras and cultures, at risk to their lives?

Finally, the type of great creative minds glorified in this book—Socrates, Michelangelo, Copernicus, Galileo, Darwin, Pasteur, and others similar to them—how many were supported by powerful social institutions of the day, and how many resisted? How many of the great ideas that significantly advanced mankind's understanding were nurtured in the cauldron of social conflict? Independent minds have suffered incarceration, decapitation, and the pyre because of uncompromising commitment to their own unique vision, and unbowed stature toward authority. Can it justly be said that any of these individuals were "molded" or "made" by their societies?

So-called "social conditioning" cannot explain autonomous thinkers who pioneer new theories and/or creations in the face of withering social opposition.

Such creators make choices; often in the teeth of daunting social repression; sometimes to the immense betterment of the human race. "Man..." said Ayn Rand, "is a being of self-made soul."[77]

Here, too, A Challenge to Determinism stands. It is easy enough to talk regarding social conditioning and its causal role in "making" an individual what he/she is. But the specific conduit between a person's family upbringing and/or education and/or religious/political indoctrination, on the one hand, and his/her thoughts, values, and actions, on the other, must be demonstrated. To explain the step-by-step causal mechanism by means of which one necessitates the other, and renders impossible countervailing thoughts, values, and actions—constitutes a task never undertaken by determinists, much less accomplished. And yet, if determinism is true, then such a step-by-step causal process is part of reality and susceptible to demonstration.

For example, let us say there is a modern-day Benjamin Franklin-type individual—reared in a Puritan family (or a strict religious equivalent). As a teenager, he/she flees to another locale of more relaxed religious instruction, sets up independently of family, becomes in time a Deist (or embraces some other form of largely secular philosophy) and, over the extended decades of a long and rich life, becomes a wealthy businessman, an accomplished prose stylist, a groundbreaking scientist, and a revolutionary statesman. An individual rebelling against family, religious mores, and the legal system—here, for a doughty determinist, is a perfect case study under the rubric of A Challenge to Determinism.

What were/are the specific steps and processes by means of which Franklin's environment and social conditioning made him (or another independent thinker) the unique individual he was—and made impossible his development into a man of contrary values?

Or, to reprise an earlier question in a new form: What are the specific steps and processes by means of which my upbringing necessitate that I 1. write a defense of free will and 2. experience myself, by means of introspection, to have a choice in the matter?

That so many individuals so often controvert family, governmental, and/or social conditioning, becoming their own man or woman, constitutes an insuperable difficulty for social determinism, and goes to the heart of this book: In advancing human knowledge and life, heroes often stand up against their family and the society of their day.[78]

The Errors of Compatibilism

In recent times and continuing to our day, the theory known as "compatibilism" is widely debated among philosophers. The essence of the theory is that free will is compatible with determinism: Because free will, in logic, is a necessary condition of moral responsibility, the theory is often upheld as the compatibility of moral responsibility and determinism.

A secondary but still important error of the theory is that, in fact, moral responsibility is not compatible with determinism.

If, for example, a gusting wind sweeps Bill McCoy off his feet, hurtles him into Joe Johnston, smashing Johnston's head against a brick wall and killing him, McCoy is guilty of neither assault, murder, nor any crime. Conversely, if he steps deliberately into Johnston's path, seizes his lapels in both hands, and volitionally crashes his head into the same brick wall, killing him—he is a murderer.

The first event is a tragic accident. The causal agent is a powerful wind. McCoy neither chose nor sought nor initiated the action. Rather, he is acted upon by an irresistible force of non-human nature.

The second event is a murderous crime. Bill McCoy, in this case, did choose, seek, and initiate the action. He, not any force independent of his will, is the causal agent.

In the first case, McCoy is not morally responsible; in the second case, he is. In the first case, McCoy should be neither censured nor punished; in the second case, he deserves both.

If the future, including human events, has but one course to the exclusion of all varying alternatives, then neither human beings nor any other agent select their actions from a range of possibilities. They do not self-enact the deeds they perform; rather, causal agent x actuates their deeds (whether causal agent x is a powerful wind, God, the devil, a person's genetic wiring, or whatever).

In such case, causal agent x is responsible for the deed(s). The human being, acted upon, necessitated to perform this and no other action, helplessly incapable of performing a contrasting action, is not morally responsible.

Observe that serious philosophic sources define the relevant principles in terms that make evident the incompatibility of free will and determinism. *The Stanford Encyclopedia of Philosophy*, for example, defines free will as: "the unique ability of persons to exercise control over their conduct in the manner necessary for moral responsibility." The same source defines determinism as: "the metaphysical thesis that the facts of the past, in conjunction with the laws of nature, entail every truth about the future." The resulting implication for an individual's conduct is: "If determinism is true, there are (causal) conditions for that person's actions located in the remote past, prior to her birth, that are sufficient for each of her actions."[79]

If every action in the future is entailed by the laws of nature in conjunction with events of the "remote past," then no occurrence can be different from what it was. In such a world, no individual chooses his/ her actions from among a range of alternatives. Free will, in such a case, does not exist ... and neither does moral responsibility.

More profoundly, compatibilism addresses the wrong question. The issue is not whether free will is necessary for moral responsibility. The issue is whether free will is real.

If we are going to cognitively begin with facts of direct awareness—as we should—then we must do so inclusively. As noted above, introspection reveals to us a world as fulsome and as real as the one displayed in extrospection. Introspection opens to us a world of thoughts, of values, of emotions, of choices, of consciousness. To ignore its existence, or deny it, or claim it is identical to firing neurons and electrical discharges is to commit as fantastic an error as to claim that matter exists solely as experiences or ideas in some consciousness.

Such errors are variations on a monist theme. Introspection reveals thoughts, values, and emotions; extrospection (in study of the brain) reveals firing neurons. As shown via direct awareness, there are two phenomena—not one. The thesis that mind and body exist in intimate causal relation has abundant evidence to support it. (Try studying calculus, for example, when your body burns with fever.) But the thesis that they are identical is false. Dualism, in some sense, is true; monism, on this issue, is false.

In logic, moral responsibility depends on free will. Via direct introspective experience, free will is shown to be real.

Compatibilism is mistaken on the first issue. It does not even
address the second one.

The cause of these errors is epistemological. The compatibilist
literature is permeated by a non-inductive, overly-abstract cognitive
method so prevalent in contemporary academic philosophy; a method
that chronically treats observational facts as though, from contact with
them, one might contract venereal disease.

In the world of nature, in billions of cases, human beings choose
from a range of alternatives presented in their environment. Having
established this truth, we can dispose of sundry points raised in relation to it in the debate regarding compatibilism.

For one, that I have power over neither the laws of nature nor the
facts of history is true. But such truths, rather than restricting the
actions over which I do have power, provide a context within which
that power is exercised. For example, because of the law of gravity,
I take an elevator from the observation deck of the Empire State Building to the street rather than the quicker route of stepping over the
railing and plummeting earthwards. The alternative of the elevator or
a quick, fatal plunge is a choice between life and death. Given a desire
for continued life, the elevator is the sole option facilitating it. *Nevertheless, a choice between life and death is real. A choice between the
elevator and the death plunge is real.* Continued life requires a method
of descent that retards gravity's function, rather than one that surrenders to it. The laws of nature delimit our options; they do not abrogate
our power of choice.

Related, because the facts of history are immutable, not subject
to my discretion, I study rather than create them. Reading *The Story
of Civilization*, after all, is a different cognitive process than writing a
novel. As noted above, I choose to spend happy hours engaged in this
rather than another activity.

In truth, human volition is limited. It cannot alter or in any way affect natural laws or historical data. It is only within the natural and social world established by these inherent or antecedently-instituted truths that an individual's free will may be exercised. Succinctly put, we choose from a range of alternatives within a context made possible by the laws of nature and by the choices and activities of those preceding us.

But limitations are to be expected: For human volition is a type of causal agency—the cause of our actions—and all causal agencies are limited. A powerful hurricane, for example, might blow through a Florida city, wreaking catastrophic destruction. But, presumably, this terrestrial storm has no discernible causal impact on the fifty-three named moons of Saturn. Nor has the same hurricane any more power than does my volition to alter the law of gravity or the date on which Caesar trespassed the Rubicon. These limits are part of the nature of causation, whether a specific cause is volitionally enacted or inexorably hard-wired into inanimate matter. Such limits do not negate causation; they merely circumscribe it.

Related: That all causes are limited in effect does not necessitate an absence of power. The atomic bomb dropped on Hiroshima, for example, did little or no damage to Rio de Janeiro but devastated significant swathes of the Japanese city.

Or, to take an example more personal and closer to home: An individual in New York City, let us say, chooses to smoke two packs of cigarettes per day for forty years. That such a choice results in negligible consequence on the cockroach population of the Congo's upper reaches does not mitigate the deleterious impact it has on the smoker's heart and lungs.

Finally, the claim that an unfortunate individual suffering from brain disease and/or psychosis loses, in some sense, cognitive control over his/her actions is likely true. But here, the exception proves the rule. That some serious biological/psychological ailment is necessary to rob the unfortunate person of his healthy capacities underscores that, when healthy, he possesses those faculties.

To tweak the example: That physically healthy human beings—billions of them—have the capacity to walk is manifest. If some crippling ailment or accident turns one, tragically, into a quadriplegic, it does not follow from such heartbreak that human beings lack the power to ambulate. Rather, again, the exception and the ailment necessary to instigate it prove the rule.

Similarly, the power of healthy human beings to choose and thereby control their actions is evident in billions of cases.

The reality of human volition, to those who do not eschew direct introspective awareness in favor of theorizing almost purely deductive, is not difficult to establish.

Heroes and Free Will

The positive relationship between heroes and free will, at this point, perhaps goes without saying. But on the premise that it is better to belabor the obvious than to risk leaving an important point unstated, let it be said: The moral stature of heroes involves choosing, from among a range of contrasting alternatives, the life-advancing deeds they perform. If reality, in some form, hard-wired those actions, then a person's "epic" deeds lose any moral status and heroism is expunged.

Hearken back to the example above of a powerful wind sweeping Bill McCoy off his feet and into Joe Johnston. Let's say Shane did not choose to confront Wilson and Fletcher; instead, as he walked down the street, a sweeping gust lifted him involuntarily, crashed him into Joe Starrett's enemies, and inadvertently killed them. This last is an action as physically necessitated as the bonding of atoms into molecules—and no more heroic.

The reality of free will underlies and makes possible the phenomenon of heroism.

Endnotes

1 E. M. Standing, *Maria Montessori: Her Life And Work* (New York: New American Library, 1962), p. 85.

2 Diane Ravitch, *Left Back: A Century of Failed School Reforms* (New York: Simon and Schuster, 2000), pp. 162, 303.

3 Andrew Bernstein, "Heroes and Villains in American Education," *The Objective Standard*, Vol. 13, No. 3, Fall 2018, pp. 14–40. Available for free at www.andrewbernstein.net. Diane Ravitch, *Left Back*, pp. 162–237.

4 Lawrence Elliott, *George Washington Carver: The Man Who Overcame* (Englewood Cliffs, N.J.: Prentice-Hall, Inc., 1966), pp. 17–18.

5 *Ibid.*, p. 23.

6 *Ibid.*, p. 27.

7 *Ibid.*, pp. 45–46.

8 Alfred Lansing, *Endurance: Shackleton's Incredible Voyage* (New York: Basic Books, 2014, 1959), p. 286.

9 *Ibid.*, pp. 293–294.

10 *Ibid.*, pp. 301–302.

11 *Ibid.*, pp. 338–339.

12 *Ibid.*, p. 348.

13 *Ibid.*, p. 342.

14 Leonard Peikoff, *Objectivism: The Philosophy of Ayn Rand* (New York: Dutton Books, 1991), pp. 259–267.

15 Thomas Maugh, "Maurice R. Hilleman, 85; Scientist Developed Many Vaccines That Saved Millions of Lives," www.latimes.com/archives/la-xpm-2005-apr-13-me-hilleman13-story.html. Retrieved July 14, 2019.

16 Daniel Coyle, *The Talent Code: Greatness Isn't Born. It's Grown. Here's How* (New York: Bantam Books, 2009), pp. 11–94 and *passim*.

17 Quoted in Peter Gibbon, *A Call To Heroism: Renewing America's Vision of Greatness* (New York: Grove Press, 2002), p. 1.

18 *Ibid.*, p. 5.

19 *Ibid.*, p. 12.

20 Sidney Hook, *The Hero In History: A Study in Limitation and Possibility* (New Brunswick, N.J.: Transaction Publishers, 1992), pp. 98–99.

21 www.whatsonxiamen.com/tag-Ellen+McDonald.html. Retrieved on February 17, 2017.

22 Lawrence Reed, *Real Heroes: Inspiring True Stories of Courage, Character, and Conviction* (Wilmington, Delaware: ISI Books, 2016), p. 2.

23 Andrew Bernstein, *The Capitalist Manifesto: The Historic, Economic, and Philosophic Case For Laissez-Faire* (Lanham, Md.: University Press of America, 2005), pp. 433–434.

24 Joseph Ellis, *Founding Brothers: The Revolutionary Generation* (New York: Vintage Books, 2002), p. 145.

25 Gillen D'Arcy Wood, *Tambora: The Eruption That Changed The World* (Princeton, N.J.: Princeton University Press, 2014), p. 211.

26 Leonard Peikoff, *Objectivism: Philosophy of Ayn Rand*, pp. 284–285.

27 www.ameliaearhart.com/about/bio.html. Retrieved June 23, 2016.

28 *Ibid.*

29 Hopefully, this will soon change. https://www.nytimes.com/2019/08/12/science/amelia-earhart-search-robert-ballard.html?searchResultPosition=1. Retrieved October 27, 2019.

30 www.ameliaearhart.com/about/bio.html. Retrieved June 23, 2016.

31 *Ibid.*, Retrieved June 23, 2016.

32 Ayn Rand, "The Objectivist Ethics," *The Virtue of Selfishness* (New York: New American Library, 1964), p. 17.

33 *Ibid.*, p. 24.

34 *Ibid.*, p. 24–25.

35 www.brainyquote.com/quotes/authors/e/ernest_shackleton.html. Retrieved on July 16, 2016.

36 Letter of George Washington to George Clinton (February 16, 1778.) www.ushistory.org/us/11f.asp. Retrieved June 24, 2016.

37 Leonard Peikoff, *Objectivism: The Philosophy of Ayn Rand, op. cit.,* p. 232.

38 R.J. Rummel, *Death By Government* (New Brunswick, N.J.: Transaction Publishers, 1994), pp. 79, 91, 111, and *passim.* Before his death, based on new evidence, Professor Rummel upped his estimate of Chinese Communist murders from roughly 35 million to greater than 70 million. See the evidence provided at his former website, now maintained by the University of Hawaii Political Science Department: www.hawaii.edu/powerkills/. Retrieved July 12, 2016. See also: Frank Dikotter, *Mao's Great Famine: The History of China's Most Devastating Catastrophe, 1958–1962* (London, Eng.: Bloomsbury Publishing, 2010), *passim.*

39 Stephane Courtois, et. al., *The Black Book of Communism: Crimes, Terror, Repression* (Cambridge, Mass.: Harvard University Press, 1999), p. 597.

40 Adolf Hitler, *Mein Kampf,* tr. Ralph Manheim (Boston: Houghton Mifflin, 1943), p. 297.

41 *Ibid.*, p. 298.

42 G.W.F. Hegel, *Philosophy of Right*, trans. T.M. Knox (London: Oxford University Press, 1967), p. 241.

43 Adolf Hitler, *Mein Kampf, op. cit.*, pp. 301, 302.

44 Ayn Rand, *Atlas Shrugged* (New York: Plume, 1999), p. 1031.

45 Andrew Bernstein, "Aristotle Versus Religion," *The Objective Standard*, Vol. 9, No. 1, Spring 2014, pp. 28–48. Available for free at www.andrewbernstein.net.

46 Armand Marie Leroi, *The Lagoon: How Aristotle Invented Science* (New York: Viking Penguin, 2014), *passim*. David Lindberg, *The Beginnings of Western Science* (Chicago: University of Chicago Press, 1992), pp. 62–68. Ernst Mayr, *The Growth of Biological Thought* (Cambridge: Harvard University Press, 1982), pp. 87–90.

47 Jis.gov.jm/heroes/samuel-sharpe/. Retrieved June 29, 2016. See also Andrew Bernstein, "Black Slaves Who Could Have Been American Founders," *The Objective Standard*, Vol. 10, No. 4, Winter 2015–2016, pp. 40–46.

48 Ayn Rand, *Atlas Shrugged, op. cit.*, p. 1029.

49 Wikipedia, entry under "Antihero." Retrieved June 24, 2014.

50 *Ibid.*

51 F. Scott Fitzgerald, *The Great Gatsby* (New York: Charles Scribner's Sons: 1925), p. 182.

52 William Faulkner, *The Sound And The Fury*, ed. David Minter (New York: W.W. Norton and Company, Norton Critical Edition, 1994 [1929]), p. 48.

53 Angus Maddison, *Phases of Capitalist Development* (New York: Oxford University Press, 1982), pp. 6–7. See regarding the starvation-level poverty of pre-capitalist, pre-Industrial Revolution Europe, Fernand Braudel, *The Structures of Everyday Life* (New York: Harper & Row, 1981), pp. 73–78. Historian, Carlo Cipolla, tells us that: "People literally died of hunger, and it was not unusual to find men dead at the roadside, their mouths full of grass and their teeth sunk in the earth." Cipolla, *Before the Industrial Revolution: European Society and Economy, 1000–1700* (New York: Norton and Co., 1976), pp. 151–152.

54 There is a strong empirical correlation between freedom and prosperity. The freer an economy is, the more prosperous; the more governmentally controlled, the less prosperous. This is true for a society's poorest members, as well as for the affluent. According to one study, *the poorest members of the world's economically freest societies earn ten times more income than the poorest members of*

the most repressed societies. See James Gwartney, et. al., *Economic Freedom of the World: 2013 Annual Report* (Vancouver, Canada: The Fraser Institute, 2013), pp. 1–24, figures cited on p. 22. Further, for 20 years, the Heritage Foundation in partnership with *The Wall Street Journal* has conducted similar research. Their annually published *Index of Economic Freedom* shows a similar positive relationship between freedom and prosperity: www.heritage.org/index/Retrieved June 15, 2016.

55 Andrew Bernstein, *Capitalism Unbound: The Incontestable Moral Case For Individual Rights* (Lanham, Md.: University Press of America, 2010), p. 55. See additionally that entire chapter, "The Inventive Period," pp. 43–60.

56 Andrew Bernstein, *The Capitalist Manifesto: The Historic, Economic, and Philosophic Case for Laissez-Faire* (Lanham, Maryland: University Press of America, 2005), pp. 294–315. For a detailed account of the Soviets' massive reliance on Western capitalism, see Antony Sutton's monumental three-volume work, *Western Technology and Soviet Economic Development* (Palo Alto, California: Hoover Institute Press, 1968, 1971, and 1973).

57 Andrew Bernstein, *The Capitalist Manifesto, op. cit.*, pp. 55–161, 323–330. The theoretical explanation of this phenomenon is best provided in *Atlas Shrugged.*

58 *The Autobiography of Benjamin Franklin* (New York: Barnes and Noble, 2005), pp. 71–74.

59 *Ibid.*, p. 79.

60 Joseph Ellis, *The Quartet: Orchestrating The Second American Revolution, 1783–1789* (New York: Alfred A. Knopf, 2016), p. 48.

61 *Ibid.*, p. 49.

62 Why do Marxists ignore or denounce Sam Walton? One reason is their claim that modern American businesses become wealthy by severe exploitation of penniless 3rd World workers. But the truth is that in the poorest countries, *American firms pay wages that are eight times higher than the national average.* (Johan Norberg,

In Defence of Global Capitalism (Stockholm, Sweden: Timbro, 2001), pp. 202–203.) Western companies pay substantially higher wages and provide better work conditions than do indigenous firms because their greater capital accumulation and deployment of modern machinery enables their workers to be more productive, to create greater wealth for the company, and to thereby earn a higher salary. The moral imperative is therefore not to pressure Western companies to pay even higher wages or to abandon their 3rd World factories; it is to overthrow the repressive dictatorships responsible for the grinding poverty, to promote the principle of individual rights, and to establish political-economic liberty in such oppressed, destitute nations. Such policies will result in greater freedom and prosperity there; just as they did in Great Britain, in the U.S., in the Asian Tigers, and across the capitalist and semi-capitalist world. However, this requires much more than political-economic revolution. In many nations, it requires substantial cultural shift to a philosophy upholding reason and a political theory upholding inalienable individual rights.

63 Thomas Sowell, *Ethnic America* (New York: Basic Books, 1981), pp. 69–99, 121–124, 126–127, 219–220, and *passim*. Often, immigrants work hard to rise out of crushing poverty—and, via continued diligence at school and work, their children take the next step into middle class affluence.

64 The American Psychological Association (APA) adopted a resolution, based on a substantial (perhaps an immense) body of empirical data, upholding the efficacy of psycho-therapy in numerous and diverse forms: apa.org/about/policy/resolution-psychotherapy. aspx. (Retrieved May 12, 2016.) Related, the psychologist, Jonathan Shedler, wrote an effective essay on this theme, "The Efficacy of Psychodynamic Psychotherapy," www.jonathanshedler.com. (Retrieved May 12, 2016.) Judith Beck, daughter of Aaron Beck, one of the founders of the cognitive school of psycho-therapy, wrote a book helpful on this topic: *Cognitive Therapy Basics and*

Beyond (New York: Guilford Press, 1995). Among other books presenting real-life case studies displaying a profound positive impact of psycho-therapy are: Irvin Yalom, *Love's Executioner* (New York: Basic Books, 2012); and Virginia Axline, *Dibs In Search of Self* (New York: Ballantine Books, 1986). There are numerous others.

65 Joanne Greenberg, *I Never Promised You a Rose Garden* (New York: Signet, 1964).

66 Viktor Frankl, *Man's Search for Meaning* (Boston: Beacon Press, 2006.)

67 Irvin Yalom, *Love's Executioner, op. cit.*, p. 78.

68 Ayn Rand, "Introduction to 25ᵗʰ Anniversary Edition," *The Fountainhead* (New York: Signet, 1993), p. ix.

69 www.amazingwomeninhistory.com/madam-c-j-walker-self-made-millionaire/Retrieved on April 16, 2017.

70 Lawrence Reed, *Real Heroes, op. cit.*, pp. 93–94.

71 See her essay, "The Objectivist Ethics," in Ayn Rand, *The Virtue of Selfishness, op. cit.*, pp. 13–35.

72 http://acolumbinesite.com/eric/writing/journal.php. Retrieved on December 6, 2019.

73 Andrew Bernstein, "Heroes of Great Literature," *The Objective Standard*, Vol. 14, No. 1, Spring 2019, p. 16.

74 Ayn Rand, *The Virtue of Selfishness, op. cit.*, p. 23.

75 Ayn Rand, *The Virtue of Selfishness, op. cit.*, p. 17.

76 www.informationphilosopher.com/solutions/scientists/libet/. Retrieved December 13, 2017.

77 Ayn Rand, *Atlas Shrugged, op. cit.*, p. 1020.

78 In *The Fountainhead*, Ayn Rand provides a brilliant fictionalized account of the struggles against society often waged by revolutionary thinkers.

79 plato.stanford.edu/entries/compatibilism. Retrieved on June 3, 2018.

CPSIA information can be obtained
at www.ICGtesting.com
Printed in the USA
LVHW050426130523
746911LV00022B/142